MAKE IT WORK OR MAKE IT GO AWAY

A Handbook for DoD Program Managers

EUGENE A. RAZZETTI

authorHOUSE

AuthorHouse™
1663 Liberty Drive
Bloomington, IN 47403
www.authorhouse.com
Phone: 833-262-8899

Published by AuthorHouse 10/21/2021

ISBN: 978-1-6655-4177-0 (sc)
ISBN: 978-1-6655-4176-3 (e)

DEDICATION

This is my sixth book. Like the others, I dedicate it to my wonderful family – living and deceased, the United States Navy, where I learned first-hand about Ethics, Management, Security, and Accountability; and to YOU: the no nonsense program management professional with a great deal to do and not much time to do it.

G.R.

CONTENTS

FOREWORD

This book is an updated compendium of articles that I have written over the past several years, dealing with the effective management of Department of Defense (DoD) programs.

The basic thread that ties them together is:

1. DoD programs are, at once, the most challenging and the most vital endeavors that will take place in the United States – now and for years to come.

2. The success of these programs depends on the thoroughness and professionalism of the contracts which directs their creation and operation. DoD contracts must reflect the scope of work to be done, the measuring criteria, the governing management structure, and robust strategies of risk management, due diligence, synergy and innovation, feedback, follow-up, and accountability.

3. The same measuring criteria used to keep a program going can tell the program manager when it should be cancelled.

4. DoD programs need input and guidance from *warfighters*, whose lives depend on the programs' success.

5. The International Standards Organization (ISO) family of management and auditing standards should be implemented (as applicable) by DoD contractors and audited by DoD program managers. Currently, the standards exist in name only in most DoD contracts, and are neither understood nor assessed by DoD contracting officials.

6. "Politics" makes for bad programs and bad results; and the selection of contractors based essentially on affiliations with members of Congress can only lead to mission failure; maybe even loss of life.

I will refer often to the term "Ethical Imperative" and to the wise words of 18th century jurist Edmund Burke, who said *"The only thing necessary for evil to succeed is that good men do nothing."*

I also refer to program management *mindsets*. By that I mean developing an ongoing quest to continually evaluate and improve a program. A belief that something can always be made better.

I wish all program managers and their supporting staffs every success – the continued existence of our way of life may very well depend on it.

Gene Razzetti
Alexandria, VA

CHAPTER ONE

Auditing Program Goals & Objectives

Nine ways in which program managers and auditors can create, evaluate, and revise program and contract goals and objectives

International Quality, Environmental, and Security Management Standards require actionable and measurable goals and objectives for certification to those standards. Outside auditors evaluate them as part of a certification or surveillance audit. Forward thinking managers conduct *internal* or self-audits to the same standards, in order to identify and solve program problems routinely.

Disciplines, structures, techniques, and checklists already exist to successfully create and monitor goals and objectives – from both inside and outside. Looking at an organization from the outside is often as helpful as looking at it from the inside. Program managers need to consider auditing of contractors to an established standard, and to ensure that auditing is permitted under the terms of the contract.

Figure 1-1. Auditing Program Goals and Objectives

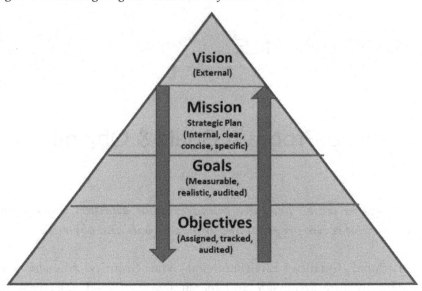

Directly or indirectly, program managers and outside auditors (like me) can audit both DoD program and contractor goals and objectives as part of normal program management and surveillance. Audits often uncover problems with the way organizations operate in the present; and, in doing so, accurately predict the future. International Standards Organization (ISO) Standards 9000, 14000, and 28000 (to name the most popular) require the presence of viable goals and objectives in order for organizations to become *ISO Certified*. They also require assessment of the organization's ability to collect and analyze data, to identify threats and assess risks, and to develop actionable corrections. They measure user feedback, the commitment of top management, and the involvement of stakeholders.

In other words, everything that a program needs to create and operate successfully.

You cannot meaningfully audit meaningless goals and objectives

You cannot meaningfully audit meaningless goals and objectives. A DoD contractor (for instance) may have stated goals and objectives that appear dazzling to the beholder, when framed and hanging in the Waiting Room or Employee Lounge. However, they often fall into several unfortunate groupings before they (just as often) fall into the trash. Realistically, many DoD program and government contractor goals and objectives are:

1. Out of date or no longer appropriate;
2. Unrealistic (i.e., too lofty, too general, or too easy);
3. Not measurable or just not measured;
4. Threatening or vindictive; or
5. Ignored and/or forgotten.

The paragraphs that follow describe nine ways to develop, revise, and audit program and contract goals and objectives.

1. Benchmarking – Where are we?

Organizations can't manage their goals and objectives without first benchmarking their circumstances. That is, determining and quantifying the *actual* performance of an operation or a process, and comparing it to *expected* performance. Benchmarking identifies the *amount* of improvement possible. Once completed, an accurate benchmarking allows program managers to assess those operations or processes on a continuing basis, in order to identify areas for improvement. Figure 2 shows the relationship between expected and actual performance. The "gap" may be strategic, tactical, or operational, depending on the matter at hand. Gap analysis comes into play here, but that's a study in itself.

Figure 1-2. Benchmarking and gap analysis

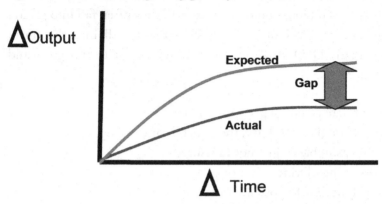

Internal benchmarking examines an organization's own activities, those taking place inside its own walls. Areas always in need of internal benchmarking include (but are not limited) to facilities, manufacturing and material handling processes, administration, training, waste, work in progress, and reject rates.

External benchmarking can include user/warfighter satisfaction, competitors' products, recommendations from external consultants and auditors, public databases, and the annual reports of other companies.

2. Synergy – Don't leave home without it

> *Synergy can be quantified. Therefore, it can be audited.*

Synergy refers to the measurable behavior of whole systems not predicted by the behavior of their component parts taken separately. Synergy can play a vital role in planning and financing global business. Industry deals with how (and to what degree) to integrate capabilities and assets of diverse component organizations and how combining the capabilities can create something greater than their total.

Organizations would do better pursuing *synergy*, rather than *innovation*, because synergy can be quantified, whereas innovation (if not the result of pursuing synergy) often cannot. It follows therefore, that if synergy can be quantified, it can be audited. What is required for the ongoing pursuit of synergies, above all, is a *mindset*. That is, a semi-automatic response from the Program Manager that says one plus one must equal 2.5 or it's not worth the doing. In business, synergy can mean that when separate departments within an organization cooperate and interact, they become more productive and efficient than if they had operated separately. For example, it is likely more efficient for each department in an organization to deal with one purchasing department, rather than for each department to maintain a purchasing function of its own. More on "mindsets' later.

Implementing synergies begins with aligning them and their associated metrics with the gaps or shortcomings discussed earlier, and for developing objectives. Threat and risk assessments, if properly conducted, should provide the required specificity for identifying the requirements and the needed synergies, and for planning.

Redundancy ➡ *Commonality* ➡ *Synergy*

In the development of synergies, Management must look for three progressively supporting behaviors:

1. **Redundancy**: wherein several organizations perform *similar* activities to achieve the same objectives; leading to
2. **Commonality**: wherein several organizations perform *the same* activities to achieve the same objectives; leading to
3. **Synergy**: wherein one organization, by *performing one activity* for several similar organizations, achieves more than could be accomplished by all the similar organizations each doing the same activity.

Too often, process improvements stop at commonality, confusing it with both innovation and synergy. Commonality is a poor substitute for either synergy or innovation.

DoD has the potential to foster a high degree of synergy. However, in terms of mission, assets, and capabilities, optimization of synergy often remains elusive. It must develop or combine material assets (weapons) and non-material assets (CONOPS) *synergistically*, in order to achieve and maintain optimal performance of systems and maximum safety, mission effectiveness, and "the most bang for the buck".

Managers and auditors must know how to look for or create synergies, how to measure their effectiveness, and how they form the basis for change and (ultimately) continuous improvement.

3. Performing a Strategy Analysis

Strategy (not *strategic*) analysis means auditing an organization at a macro, qualitative, level.

This should be considered a prerequisite to other analyses, especially as they involve Financial Management. Strategy analysis identifies profit drivers and risks, enabling auditors to assess the sustainability of current performance and to realistically forecast future performance. Strategy analysis looks at:

- ✓ Significant challenges in product, labor, or financial markets in which the organization is operating.
- ✓ Resources such as brand names, proprietary expertise, access to scarce distribution channels, and special organizational processes that create competitive advantage, and the "fit" of the organization's resources with its operations (i.e., products or services)
- ✓ Organization structure for optimal decision making and/or economies of scale (e.g., centralization versus decentralization)
- ✓ The existence of internal measurement, information, and incentive management systems, and whether they optimize operations and coordination
- ✓ The degree of rivalry among competitors and the ease with which new organizations can enter into the same market; plus the availability of substitute products and the power of buyers versus suppliers.

4. Management's External Communications

Like internal communication (e.g., within DoD), *external* communication (e.g., with investors, regulatory bodies, and the general public) should be forthright, clear, understandable, and as frequent as necessary; telling the whole story. It is safe to assume that Management will always have more timely and accurate information about the organization than will outside analysts. For that reason, there is always the possibility (accidental or deliberate) that an information "gap" will distort the organization's posture or even its solvency in the eyes of current and potential investors. Contractors must, on a continuing basis, minimize information gaps.

Management's external communications should address any differences between internal management forecasts of future earnings and cash flows and forecasts by outside analysts, and whether any differences reflect future expectations about the future of the U.S. Economy; and whether managers can credibly explain these differences. Similarly, are key business risks identified, effectively managed, and reflected in financial statements. "Unquantifiable" risks (e.g., technological innovations) must be identified and examined.

Much of a financial statement is "voluntary" disclosure. Stated another way: how much information over minimum disclosure requirements do contractors provide, in order to effectively articulate their true condition, and does the organization report sufficient free cash flow to handle (as applicable) unexpected expenses, such as to repurchase shares, or to increase dividends, and are internal or external audit reports reflected or included?

Additionally, Management can communicate with investors through meetings with financial analysts, during which it can describe current performance, strategy, and outlook for the future.

5. Risk Management – Disciplined Subjectivity

Threat x *Criticality* x *Vulnerability* = *Risk*

Organizations that implement meaningful and effective risk management programs can control both the present and the future. However, they must be able to identify the three basic components of Risk: *Threat, Criticality,* and *Vulnerability* as they apply to their organizations. Once these three components have been identified and assigned (consistent) numerical values, Management can further refine the model by "gaming" potential courses of action. It is in modeling and gaming the courses of action that Risk *Assessment* becomes Risk *Management,* as shown in figure 3.

Figure 1-3 Risk identification, quantification, and mitigation (notional)

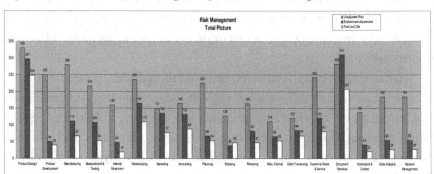

Computing Risk, in any quantifiable, consistent, and auditable manner supports evaluating management goals and objectives because risks are identified, as well as their effects and interactions. Contingency plans and courses of action can be developed, including preemptive responses which mitigate or reduce potential impacts. Additionally, expected costs can be reduced, and an appropriate balance between costs and risk exposure achieved, with the goal of reduced risk exposure.

6. Expense Analysis

> *"Inside an organization there are only cost centers.*
> *The only profit center is the customer whose*
> *check has not bounced" - Peter Drucker*

Expenses are produced from organizational resources that have either been consumed, declined in value, or been generated by marketing or advertising a product or service. Expenses also include salaries, depreciation, overhead, debt financing, taxes, and realized/unrealized declines in asset values.

Many fixed assets are "expensed" or depreciated over a period of years. That has long been a sound practice, as long as the predicted useful life of the asset is consistent with actual usage. For example: a piece of equipment may be being depreciated over a ten year period. However, the addition of a second or third shift during the second year of operation may now have it running 24/7. Auditors look for situations like this, to ensure that expenses, as managed by the organization and as reported in financial statements accurately reflect actual situations. Anything else misrepresents the situation and damages the credibility of decisions, not to mention that of both the organization and the auditor.

Program managers can provide a valued (if not always welcomed) contribution when they ensure that contractors accurately and completely measure and analyze expenses, and then share findings with internal and external stakeholders.

7. Cash Flow Analysis – Where's it all going?

Cash flow analysis examines the *quality* of the information shown on the organization's income statement, balance sheet, or cost proposal, and not just the *quantity*. Organizations normally classify their cash flows according to Operations (sales of goods and services after costs); Investments (capital expenditures, acquisitions, sales of long-term assets); and Financing activities (cash raised from ((or paid to)) stockholders and debt holders).

It can reveal the strength of the cash flow generation processes, the ability to meet short term obligations, and the amount of money that has been invested in growth. It can also reveal whether or not dividends were paid, and by what means; the type of external financing the organization relied upon; and if there was excess cash flow after making the capital investments.

It also monitors contractor business operations, growth strategy, and its financial policies. Cash flow trends over a number of reporting periods can provide valuable information on the stability of the organization and its management.

8. Credit Analysis – Another look from outside

Credit analysis is another area in which auditors, who may normally focus on operations *inside* the organization, need to adopt the perspective of potential and current suppliers, customers, competitors, and debt holders. Arguably, credit analysis by *outsiders* takes place constantly, and includes such situations as potential suppliers determining whether or not to do business with an organization or extend credit to it, or bankers determining whether or not to approve loan applications.

Fund managers, brokers, or individual investors must assess the soundness of an organization's securities. A raider organization will assess the viability of a merger, acquisition, or hostile takeover, and what constitutes fair value. Potential customers assess the efficacy of product warrantees, replacement part availability, servicing, upgrades, and predicted obsolescence.

Competitors routinely base their own decisions on the effectiveness of the organization in the market. Potential buyers or investors assess whether a troubled organization can be turned around, and how much time and funding a successful turnaround would require.

Performing credit analyses from the point of view of the outsider can provide DoD with excellent feedback about how contractors manage goals and objectives. Program managers and contractors should realize that analysis by actual outsiders is continuous, and they need to stay ahead of it.

9. Reputation and Credibility – Without Which Nothing

Auditing, as we all know, produces subjective as well as objective evidence of how an organization operates. Each quantifiable finding (i.e., each fact) obvious or hidden, simple or complicated, favorable or unfavorable, automatically generates a subjective finding as well (i.e., an opinion) can be a cause for comfort or a cause for concern.

A financial statement, for example, containing questionable or misleading exhibits can, in the long run, do more damage that an accurate exhibit in which the news is not good. A trend or pattern of misleading statements in any of the areas discussed in this article is a malignancy in the organization and can be fatal.

If a contractor has a credibility problem, reports of any type or title will be viewed with skepticism, questioned, and likely disregarded. Deliberate falsifications and "creativity" can subject creators to legal as well as administrative action. At a minimum, DoD should take its money elsewhere.

Summary

Figure 1-4 reviews where the auditing of goals and objectives fits in the big picture of program management.

Figure 1-4. Auditable goals and objectives- the big picture

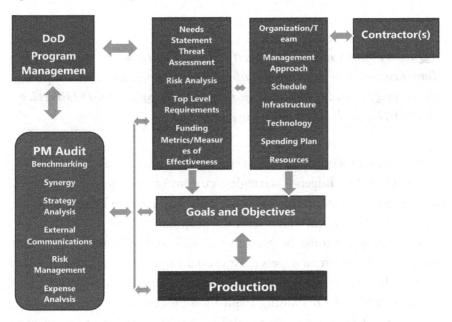

Every goal and objective must have its justification in demonstrable facts – starting with the initial benchmarking. Optimally auditing of a DoD program and its associated contractors' goals and objectives requires continual scrutiny of the many areas in which the organization performs internally and how faithfully that performance is reported externally.

Program managers, auditors, and contractors have an *ethical imperative* to ensure that their credibility remains unimpeachable. To shrink from that imperative is to travel a lonely road on a very dark night.

CHAPTER TWO

Due Diligence – Just "Due" It

> *"Quality products that <u>satisfy</u> user needs with <u>measurable</u> improvements to mission capability and operation and support, in a <u>timely</u> manner at a <u>fair and reasonable price</u>" DoD Directive 5000.1 (Underlining added for emphasis)*

Successful DoD acquisitions are the product of comprehensive, structured, and ongoing due diligence strategies, custom tailored for each phase of each program. Program managers are only half-right to believe that due diligence is *reactive,* and starts with the proposal.

Due diligence must be *proactive* as well and start with the Needs Assessment. Program managers must exert an equal level of industry when initially identifying needs and developing the requests for proposals; and then throughout the remaining acquisition process.

Figure 2-1 contains a generic DoD acquisition process, suggesting to program managers that there is both a need and an opportunity for due diligence at every program phase.

Figure 2-1 Due diligence in every step

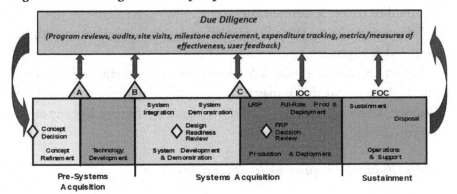

A. General

Management books define due diligence as "investigation by or on behalf of an intended buyer of a product or service to check that the seller has the desired assets, turnover, profits, market share positions, technology, customer franchise, patents and brand rights, contracts and other attributes required by the buyer or claimed by the seller."

In the private sector, designated due diligence personnel (e.g., a team of financial, technical, and/or legal experts) review and analyze all operative documents submitted by potential contract awardees. Moreover, growing numbers of business enterprises are pursuing additional legal protection for themselves so as to shield themselves from harm if their due diligence efforts fail to uncover serious problems with mergers or purchase transactions.

For our purposes, due diligence means making certain that all the facts regarding an organization are available and have been measurably verified. More on this later.

Effective due diligence processes include *Environmental* due diligence, like environmental site assessments to avoid liability under the Comprehensive Environmental Response, Compensation, and Liability Act (CERCLA), commonly referred to as the "Superfund law". *Manufacturing* due diligence contains a number of concepts involving either the performance of source inspections or surveillances, the performance of quality system audits. Due diligence in *contractor quality* is the effort made by safety, quality, and environmental professionals to validate conformance provided by sellers to purchasers. *Investigative* due diligence involves a general obligation to identify true root causes for non-compliance to meet a standard or contract requirement.

Failure to make the due diligence effort may (and perhaps should) be considered negligence.

Performing due diligence *audits* is very similar to conducting any other audit. I advise clients that it may be less complicated just to think of Due Diligence as a part of their day-to-day management strategy, like any other internal control.

B. Identifying the requirement – first things first

DoD cannot expect contractors to create spot-on products or actionable services unless it is precise in the development and specification of its requirements. The Needs Assessment and the research it both entails and generates impose ongoing due diligence demands and expectations on DoD. Only the most scrupulous developmental processes will do for the "Buy or Cancel Decision" and a flawed Statement of Work will inevitably produce a flawed product or service. See figure 2-2.

Figure 2-2 Due diligence throughout the acquisition

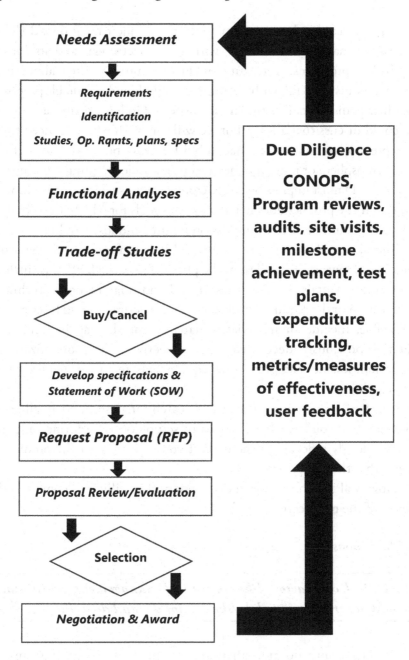

All this *before* the contractor even gets a peek at the Request for Proposal.

C. The Request for Proposal

A great deal has been written about the Request for Proposal (RFP) process, primarily having to do with the Government and its formal acquisition programs. You can find just as much written about how contractors answer RFPs with (seemingly) credible and executable proposals and their plans to achieve the success expected following contract award. We could discuss that all day, but we will stay with what you need to do to impress upon contractors that to bid for DoD business is to perform in an atmosphere of <u>mutual honesty</u>, <u>mutual understanding</u>, and <u>mutual benefit</u>. DoD must impress on contractors its seriousness and commitment, and that if the product does not achieve the goals for which it was built, a heavy cost could be exacted in mission failures and losses of life.

The size and complexity of the RFP is a function of the work requested. However, regardless of the physical size, the RFP must include many fundamentals, each well-researched and unambiguous. Technical specification of the required product or service desired should be as precise as possible. Include an abbreviated management plan, again containing material previously developed (e.g., objectives), plus organizational responsibilities, interfaces, reporting requirements, regulatory requirements, and schedules.

The RFP is the sum of all the research, analyses, and intelligence collection that you have done. It must be scrupulously performed and just as scrupulously reflected in the RFP, if you expect to get the product or service that the troops need.

How well the contractor understands and is willing to comply is the subject of the next section.

D. The Proposal

An ethical contractor, like an ethical management consultant, should never bid on a job he/she cannot do, and do well.

Proposals must do more than answer the mail – they must answer the *need*.

Upon receipt, the contractor (hopefully) will analyze the RFP thoroughly to determine whether it is to his/her advantage to respond with an offer of work. The contractor's proposal should address every point of your RFP, in accordance with the provisions that you have stated.

Some companies have business development personnel ready to respond to *any* RFP, either by themselves or with a staff of nameless, faceless, "cut and paste" commandoes. Resulting proposals are often mosaics of favorite blurbs from previous proposals. The objective: get the contract first, and then worry about how to perform the work. Be afraid, be very afraid!

Proposals require the greatest possible due diligence from both the contractor and the (DoD) program manager. Review must go far beyond block-checking and page-counting by cubicle-dwelling snuggle bunnies. Proposals must be more than just correct and comprehensive. They must be forthright, straightforward, and free of deception, credible beyond question, and must scrupulously reflect the state of the contractor's organization and management approach. The Proposal is "cradle to grave"; it should describe the entire life cycle of the product or service.

The Statement of Work must be as you wrote it, but now with the contractor's description of how they will perform your tasks. This is critical. The proposal must be responsive to the DoD's needs as specified in the RFP, complete with performance requirements and measures of effectiveness.

The Management Approach – again restating yours but with the contractor's execution plan, specifies that the design process (if appropriate) is adequately defined and incorporates appropriate technologies, such as computer aided design (CAD); databases are comprehensive and test and evaluation procedures are established or confirmed, and lifecycle requirements are defined.

A comprehensive proposal also should include (in some format or another):

- ✓ A quantifiable summary of the organization's performance track record with similar projects
- ✓ Adherence to statutory and regulatory requirements
- ✓ A vision of the outcome
- ✓ Products and services and their end use
- ✓ Comparison of the organization's products and services with those of potential adversaries

- ✓ Warranties, guarantees, and follow-on service
- ✓ Synergies and innovations
- ✓ A formidable understanding of the threat necessitating the product or service and whether the products or services address the threat for which they were developed
- ✓ Post-delivery service support (hotline, maintenance, complaints, upgrades, CONUS reach-back, etc.).

There should also be evidence (often separately provided) of contractor soundness and the assumptions underlying that soundness (i.e., will the contractor go under if it does not win your contract).

A contractor, in order to get the job, may under-bid (i.e., "low ball") the competition, often expecting to recoup lost money in amendments, modifications, and extensions. They often succeed, but they just as often wind up working nights and weekends "for free" because the money to pay for all those deliverables simply isn't there. Another unacceptable reaction is when the contractor assigns the work to less qualified personnel because the cost of their billable hours is less than the original personnel assigned. When this is planned at the outset, it's often called "bait and switch", and is unethical. In any event, you risk getting a low-quality product or service – not what you are paying for. Worse yet: not what the troops need.

When the contractor complains to his/her congressman, you really have to have your act together.

Review the proposal carefully, to ensure that you will be getting exactly what you asked for within the time, funding, quality, and performance constraints you stated – before you sign on the dotted line.

E. The execution

From the first moment of the acquisition process, program managers operate in a "triple threat" environment, as gloomily described in figure 2-3. *Performance* is critical, and the reader is reminded that there should be no doubt in anyone's mind about what the product is supposed to do. That's why the Concept of Operations (CONOPS) and the Statement of

Work (SOW) must be scrupulously developed, understood, and followed. *Time* and *cost* often have an inverse relationship with *performance.* That is, the contractor often wants more time and funding, in return for lower product expectations.

Figure 2-3 The triple threat environment

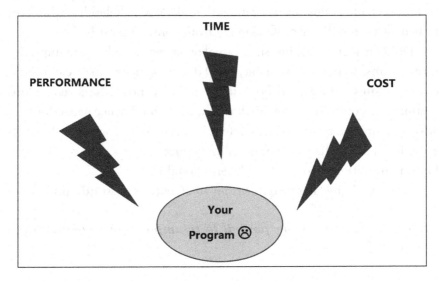

Again, program success in the triple threat environment requires due diligence in your internal controls – constant and unwavering.

Credible organizations, military and civilian, require comprehensive and meaningful internal controls. A due diligence *audit* of these controls should judge not only the *products* of the controls (e.g., records and reports), but also the *sufficiency* and *comprehensiveness* of the controls themselves, and the level of importance and relevance attached to them by the contractor. Private sector organizations that let their internal control processes slide, or do not take action on problems surfaced by the controls, deservedly lose their credibility, maybe even their existence.

You may need to bring in some outside help, with specialized experience, expertise, or certification.

Summary

Many organizations in both the public and private sectors undertake the due diligence process with insufficient vigor. In some cases, the prevailing culture (read: malaise) views it as a perfunctory exercise to be checked off quickly. In other instances, the outcome of the due diligence process may be tainted (either consciously or unconsciously) by stakeholders who stand to benefit personally or professionally from contract awards.

DoD must guard against such casual or flawed attitudes from impacting its programs. A robust, actionable, DoD due diligence strategy can prevent costly failures – measured both in lives and funds. Moreover, failures and/or shortcomings in one mission area (e.g., intelligence collection) can adversely impact related missions (e.g., power projection) as well. Those same failures will have profound consequences not only on our security, but on our national posture and international reputation.

I close with my favorite quote from 19th Century jurist Edmund Burke:

"The only thing necessary for evil to triumph is for good men to do nothing."

CHAPTER THREE

Corporate Responsibility Management and the DoD Contract – Ten Concealed Gages of a Serious, Responsible, Contractor

The most scrupulously researched and carefully worded DoD request for proposal is only as good as the contractor that wins the award. And what does DoD really know about the "winner", other than he can repeat our demands as if he created them, "cut and paste" with the skill of a concert pianist, and produce a raft of resumes for any real or imagined proficiency.

We all understand that prospective DoD contractors must provide DoD with a measurably high-quality product or service, <u>on time and within budget</u>. Good luck with that, but wait: it gets worse. Additionally, contractors today must succeed simultaneously across a spectrum of previously hidden challenges that impact the final product, regardless of whether or not they should. Such previously hidden indicators include community responsibility, employee health, safety, quality of life, and environmental compliance. More than ever, DoD contractors (like the rest of the working world) need to recognize and accept all of the previously invisible responsibilities that involve good citizenship. Fulfilling those responsibilities is neither easy nor automatic; and it will impact the final DoD product throughout its lifecycle. Accordingly, program managers should look for the key indicators discussed below in their initial contractor screenings and throughout the duration of the contract.

In recent years, even the most overconfident CEOs have acknowledged the success of structured management systems like ISO 9000, ISO 14000, and many of the others. In those same recent years, monumental company failures have both underscored the need and created the requirement for CEOs and CFOs to satisfy themselves and attest in writing regarding the veracity of their documentation. Reliance on outside auditors, to the exclusion of internal auditing and controls, inevitably leads to disaster.

In 2006, I co-created MVO 8000, an international standard for Corporate Responsibility Management. It was not the intention to replace the knowledge and skill of an ethical CEO with a cookbook. Rather, it was to provide CEOs with useful tools to run their organizations as sound, evenhanded, leaders, managers, and neighbors.

I have written for DAU about "Synergy and Innovation," "Due Diligence," "Tabletop Exercises" and the "Ethical Imperative to cancel ineffectual DoD programs". This chapter supports those other writings and describes essential indicators of Corporate Responsibility Management or CRM – a management methodology that is (sadly) not yet assessed in the DoD proposal process.

Ethical literacy ⟶ *Sense of Obligation* ⟶ *Formal Standards*

Here are ten "concealed" but measurable gages of contractor readiness and potential performance.

1. Corporate Ethics and Organizational Character

Corporate ethics concerns systemic reflection on the rules and issues of the ways in which people act. A robust Corporate Ethics or Corporate Responsibility Management program institutionalizes ethical rules and practices in the conduct of the business of a corporation. For our purposes, Corporate Responsibility Management is the creation and control of processes which ensure that DoD contractors perform to established standards of ethical practice.

Unlike the more familiar structured management approaches, CRM works with an organization's *character* rather than of its *product*; in order to establish and continually enhance the total organization and the way that it does business. Specifically, the organization's ability to:

- ✓ Create a corporate culture that promotes ethical conduct and makes it a way of life
- ✓ Make a promise and keep it
- ✓ Pledge to a compliance requirement and meet it
- ✓ Be open and honest in all its dealings, with no trade-offs or cut corners
- ✓ Show the greatest possible respect to employees and customers
- ✓ Take seriously its responsibility to the community – however large or small
- ✓ Practice environmental husbandry and conservation
- ✓ Practice responsible risk management and measurably define acceptable risk
- ✓ Develop meaningful metrics and performance indicators
- ✓ Bullet-proof customer relationships with a solid reputation
- ✓ Effectively self-audit, and not rely on outsiders
- ✓ Apply this organizational character to the future in both strategic planning and the selection and development of its next generation of leadership.

2. An Organized Corporate Responsibility Management System

Corporate Responsibility Management policy development should:

- ✓ Clearly state management's commitment to high standards of ethical practice
- ✓ Be consistent with management's vision and strategies for the future
- ✓ Permit measurable objectives to be developed
- ✓ Be widely disseminated within the organization and among other stakeholders
- ✓ Document its objectives clearly and be reviewed routinely, and be the object of continual improvement.

A structured Corporate Responsibility Management System (CRMS) covers relevant ethical aspects of business practice. Customers, suppliers, personnel, investors, and other "stakeholders" want to deal with trustworthy organizations that conduct business with integrity. A reputation for trust and integrity is an irreplaceable management asset for recruiting and retaining high quality personnel. A structured CRMS provides organizations with an agreeable, reliable, and ethically responsible working environment, providing the foundation for profitability and longevity. Not only will organizations be improved internally, but communities will be strengthened and enhanced. I see this routinely with my clients in the private sector.

CRMS implementation requires an organization to formulate policies from which relevant procedures and standards are developed. Policy statements then transition into measurable goals and objectives. Feedback mechanisms (such as internal audits and management reviews) keep the system dynamic, flexible, and self-correcting.

Formal risk assessments identify and prioritize where actions are required (or may have been ineffective). Relevant metrics monitor and measure interdependencies, and evaluate the effectiveness of preventive and corrective actions.

A CRMS is not intended for the enhancement of, or change to, the statutory and regulatory requirements to which organizations must comply, nor is it meant to replace occupational safety and health, or environmental compliance conventions. However, a CRMS, set up within an organization, can reinforce and give great credibility and cohesion to those areas.

3. Moral Values and Moral Responsibility

For simplicity, we can define moral values as the attaching of priority, importance, and allegiance to that which is morally good and correct. Having identified and stated our moral values, we need then to impose upon ourselves the responsibility to act in accordance with those moral values; specifically, the manner in which we conduct our business in the community and in the world.

4. Responsible Business Practices

Figure 3-1 describes the merging of Best Management and Responsible Business practices.

Best management practices, over the years have generally come to mean what works best for the organization. They can refer to products, services, or the indirect operation of the organization. Best management practices, like processes developed under ISO 9000 for example, should be subject to review with thought to continuous improvement through periodic review and revision. Subjecting these practices to cost-benefit analyses, or with thought to the environment (e.g., cradle-to-grave supply chain management) will likely cause their periodic revision, even if only slightly.

Figure 3-1 Merging Best Management Practices with Responsible Business Practices

The objective of *Responsible Business Practices* is to ensure that companies balance productivity and efficiency with corporate responsibility, environmental attention, and community responsibility. DoD should suspend business with unprincipled or corrupt suppliers and/or their subcontractors, including those who fail to maintain a safe and intimidation-free working environment or an effective environmental management program.

Reviewing and reassessing best management practices with thought to

Corporate Responsibility Management will likely result in some revision of those practices to the betterment of the organization and the community, as well as the final DoD product or service.

5. Vulnerability Assessment

Like any of the more conventional subsets of organizational management, corporate responsibility management should be subject to ongoing identification and assessment of vulnerabilities from within and from outside.

Figure 3-2 is a generic vulnerability assessment that CEOs or management consultants develop to show a snapshot status or situation. In doing the assessment we assume that vulnerabilities will always exist and that aggressive CRM programs can decrease their magnitude and "harden" the organization. Accordingly, the goal of vulnerability assessment is to identify areas of low process protection and strengthen them as needed.

Figure 3-2 Vulnerability Assessment

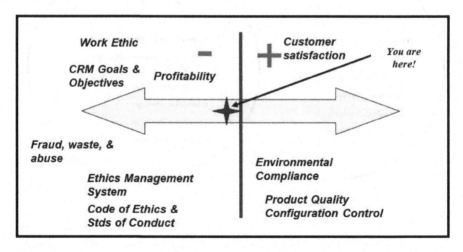

6. Converting Identified Gaps into Goals and Objectives – The Strategic Plan

There have been many excellent books written on the subject of Strategic Planning, and just as many that are trendy rather than excellent, and many consultants have been made rich ruining conference room walls with butcher paper and ink from magic markers. It is not my purpose to repeat or contradict any of them. CEOs decide the best approach; just ensuring that there is a clearly defined mission, a vision of how to accomplish the mission and with all gaps identified. This requires buy-in at all levels.

The ability of an organization to detect, react to, and correct shortcomings is one of the best ways to influence stakeholders. Whether you call them internal audits, reviews, controls, or (if you've done some time in the military) inspections, these self-imposed forays into how an organization does its business are among the single most important actions taken to keep organizations safe, legal, profitable, and responsible. Internal audits (let's use that term) let CEOs find the shortcomings before they become obvious on the outside. They can be as complex or as basic as they need to be. It's only important that they fully address all processes and that the shortcomings uncovered be acted upon. Internal auditors should not be auditing their own work, but they should fully understand the subject matter that they are reviewing.

7. Doing things Right

Sound *ethical* practices and sound *economic* practices are not mutually exclusive. In the 1990s, many companies found that environmental *management,* not environmental *compliance,* lead to better looking bottom lines as well as better looking neighborhoods. An organization intent on "doing things right" must make that intention actionable across a broad spectrum of its activities. Making a profit (as a likely example) means making that profit ethically and responsibly.

Specifications need to be correctly developed and followed; prices correctly determined; cost figures accurate and proper; and milestone inspections being performed and satisfactorily, with shortcomings identified.

Personnel training and competence must be appropriate for the tasks and the environment (if not enhanced) is not being damaged.

To achieve and maintain a reputation for doing things right, contractors must ensure that all of the above considerations (and more) are reflected in delivery of products and services.

Add to this the need to be a good neighbor. These days, many top organizations are mobilizing their forces into measurable performances of citizenship and commitment (e.g., adopt a school, park, team, or street).

8 An Ethics Mindset

Day-in/day-out allegiance to Corporate Responsibility Management starts at the top – by example and not by fiat. Nothing spells disaster more precisely than when employees see bosses breaking rules that they would break at the cost of their jobs.

Doing things right, as mentioned earlier, requires sensitivity for the ethical issues inherent in an organization or program. Contractors encounter these every day, when dealing with:

- ✓ Responsibilities to DoD
- ✓ Responsibilities to suppliers
- ✓ Employee performance measurement and handling grievances
- ✓ Benchmarking ethical performance
- ✓ Product and service quality
- ✓ Community responsibilities
- ✓ Protecting the environment
- ✓ Employee recruitment, training, competence certification, health benefits, and general quality of life
- ✓ Strategy development, marketing and sales campaigns
- ✓ Business development
- ✓ Development and certification of financial statements and disclosures.

Organizations need to develop and publish what they consider to be ethical conduct by employees at all levels. Table 3-1 is a section from the checklist for a Code of Ethics and Standards of Conduct.

Table 3-1 Code of Ethics and Standards of Conduct (segment)

Has management created a Code of Ethics and Standards of Conduct include:

- o **The Corporate Responsibility Management System,**
- o **Statutory and regulatory requirements,**
- o **Formal standards of performance and expectations,**
- o **The organization's moral values with respect to personnel customers, competitors, suppliers, and society,**
- o **Unacceptable ethical behavior as it applies to the organization,**
- o **Legal obligations of the organization and its members,**
- o **Intellectual property,**
- o **Physical and environmental security,**
- o **Access control,**
- o **Communications and operations management**
- o **Use of company property,**
- o **Internet usage,**
- o **Timesheet and travel claim preparation,**
- o **Working from home,**
- o **Internal Auditing process?**

9. Laws, Regulations, and the Environment

> *"To expect no regulation is willful blindness"* – Peter Drucker

We have had a history of manufacturing crises in the U.S. – unsafe automobile brakes, tires, and air bags, air and water pollution, improper hazardous waste disposal, and squandering of public utilities. This history has been chronicled in terms of deaths, diseases, public scandals, fines, product removals/recalls, and company bankruptcies; and also, by Government investigation, intervention, and legislation. When the Government gets involved, it is usually after the damage is done and punitive action is the order of the day. It does not have to be that way, and forward-thinking organizations know that. The public in general and DoD in particular has the right to expect its products not only to be safe but to cause no harm in their creation; and the Government has the obligation to ensure that right.

DoD contractors need to identify their environmental impact(s) — actual and potential, positive and negative. An organization implementing a Corporate Responsibility Management System and not yet having an Environmental Management System can create both simultaneously. The organization should benchmark its initial situation relative to environmental compliance. It can effectively do this by conducting an assessment of its environmental compliance status with regard to:

- ✓ Hazardous material control and management
- ✓ Its activities and processes and their environmental impact
- ✓ Applicable statutory and regulatory requirements
- ✓ Pollution prevention and energy conservation
- ✓ Supplier selection
- ✓ Contract development
- ✓ Identification and monitoring of environmental aspects.

10. Outreach into the Community

Contractors should fully define and accept their roles, responsibilities, and authorities as members of the community, to include:

- ✓ The potential of all operations on the environment
- ✓ Periodically evaluating performance of community responsibilities as part of the a formal review process, appropriate feedback mechanisms, and normal and emergency lines of communication.
- ✓ Execution of environmentally sound policies and objectives
- ✓ Developing recommendations for improvement.

Summary

At this point, we know that black ink on the bottom line is not enough. There are other considerations and measurements of a DoD contractor. If the elements of an effective CRMS are not there, sooner or later the product suffers.

DoD contractors need to identify all the processes of the potential product or service. Once identified, then to understand the inherent risks to the product and the environment. Product performance must be capable of measurement, and the findings actionable. Core values need to be in writing – in the base documents and all supporting documents as well.

DoD contractors need to identify all stakeholders. Certainly, they include the military end user; but also, employees, suppliers, shareholders, and surrounding communities. Stakeholders may be scattered all over the world, or just downstream of that little creek that flows behind the loading dock. Contractors can communicate through a very sophisticated website or through the storm drains.

Program managers and contractors need to identify all the ethical issues associated with contract performance. Contractors need to recognize their obligation to deliver value and the direct relationship their reputation has with that value. Contractors put their names on their product, whether they realize it or not.

Day-in/day-out allegiance to a Corporate Responsibility Management System starts at the top – by example and not by fiat. A DoD contractor's responsibility to its employees and suppliers goes beyond writing checks. They have an obligation to be fair and honest with them and a right to expect the same in return.

CHAPTER FOUR

Compliance, Continuity, and COVID - The DoD Missions Continue, regardless – And Remotely

The COVID-19 Pandemic, also known as the Coronavirus Pandemic, is an ongoing contagion of coronavirus disease 2019 (COVID-19) producing severe acute respiratory syndrome coronavirus 2 (SARS-CoV-2). First identified in December 2019 in Wuhan, China, the outbreak was declared a Public Health Emergency of International Concern in January 2020 and a pandemic in March 2020. As of 6 November 2020, more than 48.8 million cases worldwide have been confirmed, with more than 1.23 million deaths attributed to COVID-19.

> *When the pandemic hit, fewer than 50% of US companies had a generic contingency plan and 10% had no plan at all.*

Whether an organization was well-prepared for a pandemic or it had no contingency plan in place, business disruption and disaster followed. Organizational leaders saw firsthand the fragility of business systems, operations and revenue streams witnessed the critical importance of risk awareness and preparedness, as well as the need for robust "Continuity Management" programs.

Today, DoD program managers and contractors face a dual challenge: (1) How do they ensure continuity in their programs before during, and after a major disruption such as a pandemic; and (2) How do they do it remotely. If it helps create a sense of urgency for program managers: think of COVID 19 as a *bio-weapon*.

This is the second of two articles on working through the COVID 19 Pandemic. This article discusses the importance of Continuity Management in both the public and the private sectors. Like the cyberattack threat, the Pandemic threat will forever be real; and DoD's response to it must be just as real.

> **Compliance without Continuity is worthless in a pandemic**

Compliance with the applicable DoD contract is (or should be) mandatory for contract award and execution. However, *compliance* alone doesn't guarantee the ability of an organization to successfully respond to and survive a major disruptive incident; especially one with the scope, duration, and severity of the COVID 19 Pandemic.

Compliance with contract specifications can (to some extent) provide the Program Manager with a good feeling about the contractor's past, and a good snapshot of the contractor today; but *not nearly enough about tomorrow.* That kind of good feeling comes only with a favorable assessment the contractor's ability to handle "tomorrow." In short: Compliance requires Continuity. Otherwise, there may not be a "tomorrow" for the program. No "new normal;" or any other kind for that matter.

Figure 4-1 describes the sequence from "normal" to "new normal," and the importance of continuity planning to recovery and restoration.

Figure 4-1 Continuity planning

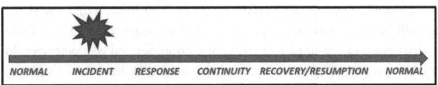

NORMAL   INCIDENT   RESPONSE   CONTINUITY   RECOVERY/RESUMPTION   NORMAL

I have written articles for DAU on the following distinct but related subjects over the last several years:

- Contingency Planning
- Adding COVID 19 to your Risk Management Model

- Collecting and analyzing "Lessons Learned"
- The importance of Second-Party Auditing
- Cybersecurity and System Integration in DoD
- Due diligence in DoD contracts and the courage to cancel a failed DoD program
- Lessons learned from Afghanistan
- Second party auditing of DoD contracts
- The value of Tabletop exercises.

When initially published, those articles were meant to help focus program managers on maximizing the effectiveness of both their programs' missions and their administration of them. Now, in light of the pandemic, my hope is that revisiting them will help to focus program managers on rebuilding programs damaged by the Pandemic; and to rebuild and operate them *remotely*, as the situations require.

Same challenge – different distance

The following terms will also help to assess continuity for future recoveries and structure the rebuilding required for recovery operations already in progress.

Continuity, for our purposes, means the ability to deliver previously agreed products and services even under extremely negative situations (e.g., during or after a natural disaster, terrorist act, or massive process failure). "Delivery" may be either to internal or external parties (e.g., between processes or to the end user).

Continuity management means a management process that covers the identification of situations that may have a high negative impact on DoD operations; and the implementation of capabilities and competencies, in order to properly respond to them and to protect the interest of DoD and other relevant interested parties.

Continual Improvement is the basis and underpinning of modern management. It must be thought of as an ongoing process and not an "end state". It requires program managers and contractors to develop mindsets that we can always make something better.

Impact Analysis (IA) is a process that helps to identify the threats and effects that a disruption or serious situation can have on operations or activities. **Impact analysis helps organizations to build resiliency and responsiveness into their operations.**

A *Risk Management Plan* can be thought of as the end-user of the impact analysis. An organization's continuity management plan must have in place, a documented risk assessment process, in order to identify, analyze, evaluate, and treat risks that may lead to disruptive situations. Risk management (assessment and treatment criteria development) must consider the continuity plan's objectives and the organization's definition of acceptable risk.

Personnel awareness is an essential part of personnel competence. People who work under an organization's control must be made aware of the continuity policy and its contents, and what their personal performance means; plus, its objectives, and what the implications of nonconformities may be, and their roles during disruptive incidents. It's analogous to knowing the location and use of the closest fire extinguisher, fire alarm box, first aid kit, or eyewash station – only on a grander scale. And remotely.

Resources support continuity strategies. Organizations must define needed continuity resources, like people, information and data, buildings and facilities, equipment and consumable resources, transportation, suppliers, and partners.

Continuity Management Plan

A *Continuity Management Plan* is a set of procedures and instructions to guide an organization during and after a disruptive event; in order to speed up immediate response, recovery, and resumption of minimum operational conditions, and eventual restoration of normal operations. We must consider now the pandemic-driven requirement to assess and manage those management functions from a distance.

Table 4-1 compares normal DoD program management compliance functions with Continuity Management; then goes on to suggest that these functions may be monitored remotely. The requirements for compliance and continuity are essentially the same. It follows therefore that *continuity* in DoD programs must start at the very inception of the contract, and remain an integral part of it throughout. Normal and continuity management functions are identical; so it should not be a difficult shift to a "restoration" scenario if continuity was built into compliance at the beginning.

Table 4-1 Remotely monitoring compliance and continuity

Management Function	Compliance	Continuity	Monitor Remotely
Top management involvement	✓	✓	✓
Provision of resources	✓	✓	✓
Cost-benefit and risk analyses	✓	✓	✓
Preventive/corrective actions identified	✓	✓	✓
Internal audit	✓	✓	✓
Critical personnel/functions identified	✓	✓	✓
Recovery time objective established	✓	✓	✓
Exercise gaming (potential disruptions)	✓	✓	✓
Incident response structure	✓	✓	✓
Continual improvement	✓	✓	✓

The sections that follow expand on some of vital continuity management practices that already lend themselves to remote monitoring, and have done so for a long time.

Cost-Benefit Analysis

Cost-benefit analysis is a process with which businesses analyze decisions. The manager or analyst sums the benefits of a situation or action and then subtracts the costs associated with taking that action. Figure 4-2 describes the basic cost-benefit analysis process in action.

Figure 4-2 Cost-benefit analysis

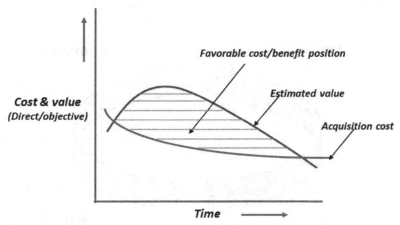

Thorough cost-benefit analyses reflect both objective (direct/easily quantified) and subjective (indirect/not easily quantified) costs and benefits. This can be done remotely, and revised whenever the situations change. Forward-thinking program managers are already doing cost-benefit analyses remotely.

Process approach

A Process Approach means managing a group of processes as a system, where the interrelations between processes are identified and the outputs of a previous process are treated as the inputs of the next one. The process approach helps to ensure that the results of each individual process will *add value* and contribute to achieving the final desired results. There should (theoretically) be no wasted or unnecessary operations. Process approaches also identify opportunities for potential synergy, innovation, risk identification, and resource reallocation. Even the most complicated processes may be analyzed and monitored remotely, with a little planning.

Figure 4-3 describes the basic process approach challenge for DoD program managers.

Figure 4-3 The basic process approach in program management

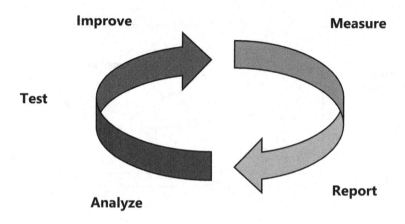

Whether you call it "Plan – Organize – Actuate – Control" as we Business majors called it in 1965; "Define – Measure – Analyze – Improve – Control (DMAIC)", if you are into Six Sigma; or "Plan – Do – Check – Act" as everybody else does, it's all the same. Your challenge *now* is that you may have to manage or audit much (if not all) of the processes from a distance.

Recovery Time Objective

The Recovery Time Objective (RTO) is the duration of time and a service level within which a program's processes must be restored after a disaster, in order to avoid unacceptable breakdowns in continuity. Often used with Information Technology (IT), RTOs can be used to measure the time it takes after the disruption to recover data.

RTOs also help to determine how long a business can survive with reduced infrastructure and services.

RTOs are often complicated. IT departments can streamline some of the recovery processes by automating them as much as possible, with tripwires and preplanned responses built into the software. A meaningful RTO involves the entire infrastructure of the organization.

Auditing – more essential than ever

An "audit" (for our purposes) is a systematic, independent, and documented process for obtaining objective evidence, and evaluating it, in order to determine the extent to which program criteria (policies, procedures, or requirements) are being fulfilled.

Many DoD contractors routinely "certify" to one or more of the International Standards Organization (ISO) Management Standards (e.g.; ISO 9001:2015: Quality Management Systems). Not only are those organizations subject to periodic audits by accredited certification bodies, but have an obligation to internally *audit themselves* in order to ensure compliance with the International Standard and maintain their certifications. Adherence to the International Standards also indirectly audits contractors to the requirements of the DoD contract.

Accordingly, program managers for these "ISO-Certified" DoD contractors have at their disposal the ability to: (1) directly audit the contractor; (2) directly assess the contractor's ability to audit itself; and (3) monitor the status of the contractors' certifications.

More than any other meaningful assessment, audits can be conducted and monitored remotely. Additionally, remote audits take less time to schedule and conduct. Remote audits eliminate budget-busting "other direct costs" such as airline tickets, hotel rooms, meals, and rental cars. Findings, feedback, and corrective actions may be faster as well, especially when working with decentralized or overseas operations or organizations.

Forward-looking certification registrars and management consultants of my acquaintance add value by offering new and existing clients *remote* audits; wherein they optimize document reviews via emails; conduct ZOOM and SKYPE conferences and interviews, and critiques; and (last but not least) use telephone cameras to remotely observe factory floors, warehouses, and loading docks.

Tabletop exercises and TACSITS

Tabletop exercises as pandemic "rehearsals"

A tabletop exercise is an activity in which key personnel assigned high-level operational and administrative roles and responsibilities gather to deliberate various simulated emergency or rapid response situations. Tabletops are used frequently to improve team responses, disaster preparedness, and emergency planning; and also contribute lessons learned to less time-critical challenges, like stateside program administration. Tabletop exercises can serve as "disruption rehearsals" by simulating actual events for preparation before, progress during, and recovery after, the simulated disruption.

Tactical Situations (TACSITS) are scenarios based on real-world conditions used to shape and forecast future operations. They give structure, substance, and direction to tabletop exercises. Computer modeling and simulation are used when insufficient data or knowledge exists. Figure 4-4 describes the creation and continuing improvement of TACSITS.

Figure 4-4 Developing a Pandemic TACSIT

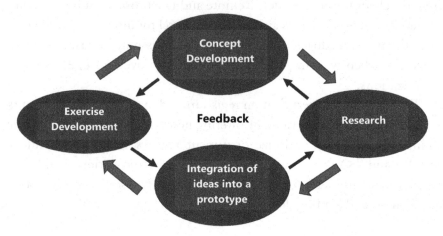

An enduring feedback loop increases productivity and potential contribution. The more remote the operation – the greater the need for real-time feedback.

A pandemic TACSIT can be as useful as TACSIT developed for a more traditional warfighting missions, such as a SEAL incursion, cargo routing, or noncombatant evacuation.

Summary

The COVID 19 Pandemic underscored the need for continuity plans and the decisions that they include; decisions that must be the product of formal, structured, and defensible processes. Otherwise, they will be as meaningless and potentially dangerous as an empty fire extinguisher.

Compliance without Continuity is meaningless, in even the most benign scenarios. Disruptions and disasters like the COVID 19 Pandemic can destroy a DoD program from all sides simultaneously.

Continuity means the ability to deliver previously agreed products and services even under extremely negative situations, such as a pandemic. Continuity plans, made up of tripwires and preplanned responses guide organizations during and after disruptive events, to speed up immediate response, recovery, and resumption of minimum operational conditions, and restoration of normal operations.

Continuity requires the same best management practices that program managers already use in every contract, program, or process; but with a greatly enhanced wariness for the unexpected. See table 4-1.

Audits, internal or external, remote or on-site, are the essence of compliance monitoring, feedback, corrective action, and continual improvement.

Tabletop exercises and TACSITS can be excellent "disruption rehearsals." They can simulate actual events for preparation before, progress during, and recovery after a disruptive event.

The Program Manager's challenge *today* is to manage many (if not all) of the programs from a distance. The good news is that most good management practices can be managed and monitored remotely, and are already being monitored remotely for decentralized and overseas organizations.

If it helps in the development of a sense of urgency for continuity planning: think of COVID19 as a "bio-weapon," employed by a formidable adversary who is intent on world domination. In fact, I highly recommend it.

CHAPTER FIVE

Building in Reliability – Get it right the first time; or as soon as you can

I have written articles urging the integration of the International Standards Organization (ISO) Family of Standards such as *ISO 9001:2015: Quality Management Systems* with the Department of Defense (DoD) Adaptive Acquisition Framework (AAF).

Numerous Government contracts currently "require" contractor certification to one or another ISO Standard, but the language of the Requests for Proposal (RFP) has been tentative and uncertain – suggesting a lack of ISO motivation, familiarity, or competence on the part of contract creators. Contractors usually recognize this, and reply to a tenuous requirement in the RFP's *Statement of Work* with a specious comeback in the proposal's *Management Approach.* Alternately, contractors hurry to "get certified" before the proposal submission deadline. As a result, both sides fulfill the letter but not necessarily the spirit of contract requirements. The end-product suffers – as do the mission and the Warfighter.

> *Whether referenced in the contracts or not, program managers can employ the ISO management practices in the day-to-day management of their contracts.*

The good news, however, is that even if DoD continues its uncertain movement to link ISO and AAF, program managers can still employ the ISO management practices in the development, implementation, auditing, and day-to-day management of their AAF contracts.

Quality and Reliability – boldly launching from a secure base

To think of "quality" merely as "conformance to specification", or (worse yet) as "in the eye of the beholder" is to think of it as static. Unchanging. One and done.

Quality is both static *and* dynamic. Since the earliest days of Fredrick W. Taylor and the Gilbreths, quality has been considered iterative, ever-changing, and the focus of continual improvement. The product or service can always be made better.

Quality textbooks in classrooms and quality manuals on factory floors emphasize making products *consistently* first and then *better* as you go along.

Determining the *quality* of a product often requires measurement with test equipment and instruments, tests and trials; and assessment and approval in the early stages of design and development; checklists and flow charts. These practices, too often considered static and distant, form the secure base and launching pad, which, if and when constructed, moves program managers boldly on to quality's more dynamic and enduring system of measurement: reliability. Many measurement tools (e.g., test equipment, calipers, and the like) are often considered static; hence the need to emphasize the dynamic nature of reliability, as we are about to do.

Reliability refers to the consistency of a measure. The reliability of a system, product, or process, is the probability that it will perform correctly for a specified period of time under specified conditions.

Consider three types of consistency: over time (test-retest reliability), across items (internal consistency), and across different researchers (inter-rater reliability). Consider reliability as the program manager's best, most telling, scheme to measure continuing, enduring, quality.

Having linked quality with reliability, it is no stretch therefore to appreciate that an increase in a product's quality increases its reliability as well, as suggested with figure 5-1. The relationship between quality and reliability shows how examining and improving one has the same effect on the other.

Figure 5-1 The direct relationship of quality and reliability

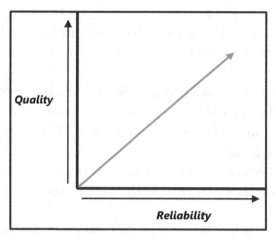

Figure 5-2 provides examples of where quality management and reliability engineering intercept and inter-react, first in the design of products or services, and later in their actual service.

Figure 5-2 Interoperability of quality and reliability

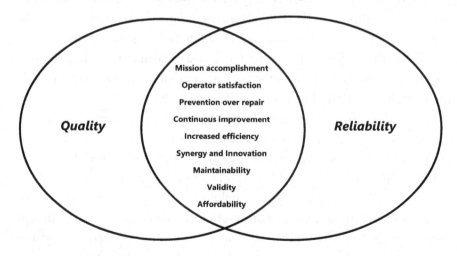

Reliability engineering (normally considered a sub-discipline of systems engineering) emphasizes the ability of equipment to function without failure. Reliability (in this context) describes the ability of a system or component to function under specified conditions for a specified period of time.

The goal of reliability engineering is to use engineering knowledge and techniques to prevent certain failure modes and to reduce the likelihood and frequency of failures; to identify and correct the causes of failures that *do* occur, in addition to the efforts to prevent them.

Reliability engineering over the long haul requires thoughtful use, understanding, and appreciation of a veritable "toolbox" of proven concepts, practices, and activities, as described briefly in the sections that follow.

Figure 5-3 The reliability engineer's toolbox

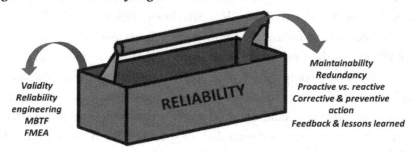

Reliability in general and reliability engineering in particular help us quantify product quality by adding the dimension of time to the quality equation. In other words, we no longer just want to know if a product can perform its intended function at the moment of purchase, we want to make sure that the product works without major malfunctions under normal conditions for as long as possible – ideally, throughout its lifecycle.

Validity is used to evaluate quality. The term refers to whether or not the test measures what it claims to measure. On a test with high validity the items will be closely linked to the test's intended focus. If a test has poor validity, then it does not measure the job-related content and competencies it ought to.

Validity should be thought of as the extent to which the scores from a measure represent the variable for which it was intended. When a measure has good test-retest reliability and internal consistency, program managers can be more confident that the scores represent what they want to measure.

Mean time between failures (MTBF) is the predicted elapsed time between inherent failures of mechanical or electronic systems during normal operation. MTBF can be calculated as the arithmetic mean (average) time between failures of a system.

The definition of MTBF depends on the definition of a *failure*. For complex but repairable systems, failures are considered to be those out of design conditions which place the system out of service and into a state of disfunction. Failures which occur that can be left or maintained in an unrepaired condition, and do not place the system out of service, are not considered failures under this definition. In addition, units that are taken down for routine scheduled maintenance or inventory control are not considered within the definition of failure. The higher the MTBF, the longer a system is likely to perform satisfactorily before failing. The term is used for repairable systems, while mean time to failure (MTTF) denotes the expected time to failure for a non-repairable system.

Failure mode and effects analysis (FMEA) is the process of reviewing as many components, assemblies, and subsystems as possible to identify potential failure modes in a system and their causes and effects. For each component, the failure modes (means) and their resulting effects on the rest of the system are recorded on specific FMEA worksheets. An FMEA can be a *qualitative* analysis, but may be put on a *quantitative* basis when mathematical failure rate models are combined with a statistical failure mode ratio database. FMEA was one of the first highly structured, systematic techniques for failure analysis. It was developed by reliability engineers in the late 1950s to study problems that might arise from malfunctions of military systems. An FMEA is often the first step of a system reliability study. A few different types of FMEA analyses exist, such as Functional, Design, and Process. Key failure modes must be quantified, reported, and corrected as soon as possible after identification.

Maintainability means the ease (or difficulty) with which:

- ✓ Product defects and their causes are corrected;
- ✓ Faulty or worn-out components can be replaced without having to replace adjacent or supporting components;
- ✓ Unexpected working conditions are minimized or prevented;
- ✓ A product's useful life, efficiency, reliability, and safety are maximized;
- ✓ New or emergent requirements are addressed;
- ✓ Future maintenance can be made easier; and
- ✓ Changing environments can be addressed.

Maintainability should be a sub-set of an overall strategy of continuous improvement - learning from the past in order to improve the ability to maintain current systems, or improve the reliability of future systems, based on maintenance experience.

Redundancy generally means exceeding what is normal. It can also refer to a person no longer needed in his/her place of employment (and about to get the axe). However, in engineering, the term is used more specifically and refers to duplicate devices that are used for backup purposes. The goal of redundancy is to prevent or recover from the failure of a specific component or system.

Redundancy occasionally results in less, instead of more reliability. A more complex system (albeit with increased redundancy) may be prone to increased issues. Also, too much redundancy may lead to delayed discovery and/or repair of the initial problem, brought on by a perceived lack of urgency (e.g.; "The system will still run from the alternate source of power"). Over-complicated production demands (on redundant components) may overstress the system and make it less reliable from a mission standpoint.

Put another way: engineering systems redundancy is about providing reliability by adding a process alternative to a failing condition. An alternative response can be designed into a system at the component level (i.e., two processors, two pumps, or two sources of power). At the process level, assuring reliability through redundancy may require two separate process trains.

As suggested in figure 5-4, a suspension bridge's numerous cables are a well-known and easily recognized example of redundancy.

Figure 5-4 A suspension bridge (where redundancy meets reliability)

Proactive vs. Reactive. Proactive means acting *before* a situation becomes a source of confrontation or crisis. To be **reactive** is to *deal with the past* rather than to anticipate the future. A proactive approach focuses on eliminating problems before they have a chance to appear and a reactive approach is based on responding to events after they have happened. The difference between these two approaches is the perspective each one provides in assessing actions and events.

Program managers and reliability engineers need to be proactive in every phase of a program's development; constantly looking for potential problems and gathering meaningful data from all sources. Achieving reliability by reactive measures can be costly, in terms of finance, delivery times, and mission success.

Corrective and preventive actions are improvements to an organization's processes to eliminate causes of failures, non-conformities, or other undesirable situations. It is usually a set of actions that laws or regulations require an organization to take in manufacturing, documentation, procedures, or systems to rectify and eliminate recurring non-conformance. Corrective actions *eliminate* the causes of existing non-conformities or other undesirable situations, so as to prevent recurrence. Preventive actions *avoid* the occurrence of potential non-conformities, generally as a result of a risk analysis.

Examples of corrective actions include (but are not limited to):

✓ Error Proofing
✓ Visible or Audible Alarms
✓ Process Redesign
✓ Product Redesign
✓ Training or enhancement or modification of existing training programs
✓ Improvements to maintenance schedules.
✓ Improvements to material handling or storage.

Reliability engineers, when developing or revising maintenance programs, must implement comprehensive (corrective and preventive) action and maintenance programs, with solid feedback networks.

Feedback is communication (in whatever form) that program managers and reliability engineers receive regarding some action the program is planning to take or has already taken. Feedback is an indispensable part of the decision-making process – whether in strategic planning, in day-to-day operations, or at the end of the mission or system lifecycle. Feedback allows program managers to identify and assess existing problems and to mitigate or avoid those same problems in the future.

Ideally, feedback means *continuous information on performance against accepted standards.*

However, before you can expect *meaningful* feedback, think about these:

✓ Your feedback requirements should be clearly stated, in writing
✓ Whatever you want done may *not* get done, if there is no feedback system in existence. Ensure therefore, that feedback mechanisms exist. If there is no established feedback system in place, you will need to create something, even if it's only temporary.
✓ Feedback is two-way; all stakeholders need to know the findings of the feedback process as much as the program manager does, so ensure they stay informed.
✓ Be alert for unexpected obstacles or surprises.

Lessons learned are findings and experiences distilled from a project, lessons that should be actively taken into account not only in future projects, but for "mid-course corrections" to current projects. Findings may be positive, as in a successful test or mission—or negative, as in a mishap or failure.

The two most serious mistakes that a program manager can make to render lessons learned ineffective (read: meaningless) are (1) to not include *warfighter/user* input; and (2) to wait until the end of the program to collect them.

Regrettably, capturing lessons learned is usually thought of as a standalone, static, act — awaiting conclusion of the program or exercise. Further, feedback, once collected, often enjoys a late launching and a limited distribution. Participants whose contribution would likely be uncomplimentary or disapproving are often not asked for to participate in the feedback process.

Figure 5-5 summarizes the feedback and lessons learned process for DoD program management.

Figure 5-5. Feedback and lessons learned

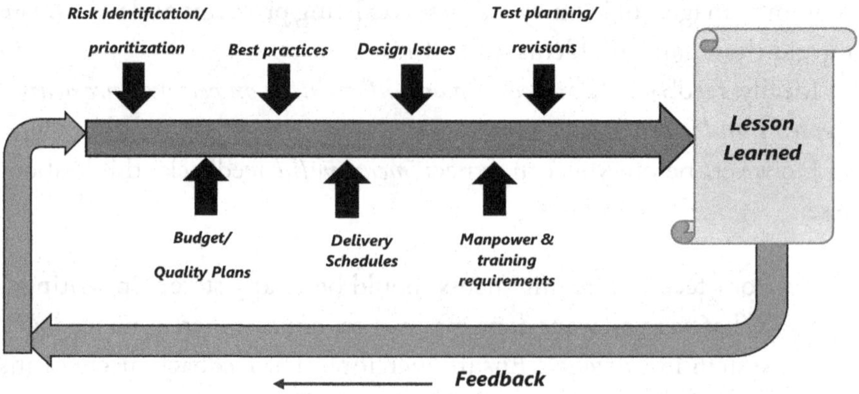

Summary

Quality is both static *and* dynamic. Something can always be made better. Even if DoD continues its hesitant movement to join ISO with AAF officially, program managers can still employ the ISO management practices in the development, implementation, auditing, and day-to-day management of their AAF-compatible contracts.

The reliability of a system, product, or process, is the probability that it will perform correctly for a specified period of time under specified conditions. Reliability dynamically describes the ability of a system or component to function under specified conditions for a specified period of time. It is the program manager's best, most meaningful, scheme to measure continuing, enduring, quality.

Program managers and reliability engineers have a formidable "toolbox" of proven concepts, approaches, and practices available to them. They need to be *proactive* in every phase of a program's development; constantly looking for potential problems and gathering meaningful data from all sources. Achieving reliability by *reactive* measures can be costly, in terms of finance, delivery times, and mission performance. Similarly, *preventive* maintenance is more cost-efficient and success-focused than *corrective* maintenance.

Feedback means *continuous information on performance against accepted standards*. Feedback in all forms is vital to a program's success. DoD must learn from the successes and failures of its programs – throughout their lifecycles.

CHAPTER SIX

System Integration - Enabling Capability Through Connectivity

Part I Program Management

In the past, I have written about program management in DoD and stressed the need for:

- Risk management and gap analysis
- Operator and/or warfighter participation in the program
- Meaningful feedback, follow-up, and accountability
- Modeling and simulation, including tabletop exercises and/or wargames

This article adds "System Integration" to the discussion, as both a component and a byproduct of successful program management. System integration is not rocket science, but it is a challenge, and, according to certain studies, up to 70 percent of system integration projects fail or fall short in some part. When program managers stay focused on system integration throughout the program, and not as an end-of-pipe activity, successful integration of subsystems into a finalized system is almost certain. The "System Integration Plan" will write, revise and continually improve itself.

> *Successful system integration employs the principles and practices of successful program management— you have to do all this stuff anyway.*

System Integration and Program Management

System Integration is the process of bringing together the component sub-systems into one system. It is an aggregation of subsystems cooperating so that the resultant system is able to deliver an overarching functionality or capability by ensuring that the subsystems function together as *one* system. In information technology, this is the process of linking together different computing systems and software applications physically or functionally, to act as a coordinated whole. An integrated system streamlines processes, reduces costs and increases efficiency.

System Integration connects multiple separate components —often from different sources—to work as one. Some subsystems are old, some are new. Program managers usually find that putting the subsystems together as early as possible in the program's development improves mission effectiveness and helps to ensure seamless *connectivity,* enabling commanders at the front and at the rear to better execute and assess strategic and tactical accomplishment.

Connectivity refers to a program's or device's ability to link with other programs or devices. For example, a program that can import data from a wide variety of sources and can export data in many different formats is said to have "good connectivity," especially when connecting to or communicating with another computer or computer system. The finest subsystems are useless (or at least fall short) if they cannot effectively connect with each other and form the system. Connectivity in decision making means harnessing information from many information generators (or sensors) into one total picture—often called the Commander's Dashboard.

System integration employs all the principles and practices of successful program management; there is virtually nothing that should be considered new, unique or *over and above.* Table 6-1 summarizes and compares the requirements of system integration with those of successful program management. The requirements are identical.

Table 6- 1. Comparing Systems Integration with Program Management

Requirement	Program Management	System Integrations
Mission planning; concept development	✓	✓
Design/development (including hardware/ software)	✓	✓
Modeling/Simulation	✓	✓
Research & development	✓	✓
Risk management plan	✓	✓
Gap analysis	✓	✓
Core team developed; responsibility/ accountability assigned (including decision makers)	✓	✓
Warfighter involvement	✓	✓
Performance-oriented; metrics developed/ consistent/actionable	✓	✓
Test plans developed; tech yield identified	✓	✓
Contract in place; executable	✓	✓
Connectivity/feedback	✓	✓
Configuration/change management process defined/in place	✓	✓
Internal/external security procedures in place	✓	✓
Life cycle management plan	✓	✓

Please note especially the inclusion of "warfighter involvement," "technological yield," and "connectivity." These requirements, often neglected in a program's early stages, are essential not only for managing the program but for ensuring that subsystems and components successfully address the mission and *integrate* into a viable end product ("e.g., a weapons system, with all hardware, software, training simulators, and supply support).

Research and Development—Another Way to Look at It

Past usage of the familiar and perhaps archaic term "Research and Development" or "R&D" has often suggested its detachment, and/or inclusion as an *end* product at the *beginning* of the design. "Acceptance testing" (an equally archaic term) often is thought to be at end of the development pipeline. Taking these approaches invites programmatic disaster.

The alternative approach shown in Figure 6-1 depicts potential gain from a robust and ongoing integration/connectivity strategy in the R&D processes, where subsystems are measured continuously against system requirements. Acceptance testing is constant and actionable feedback is immediate. *Quality* testing throughout development replaces *quantity* testing at the end; and proactive configuration management replaces recalls and retrofits.

Figure 6-1. Research and Development Connectivity

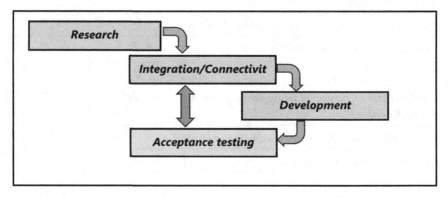

Subsystems are validated and tested. Test engineers, detecting any problems, can initiate corrective action. The subsystem again undergoes operational (acceptance) testing, to ensure that the subsystems come as close as possible to errorless performance.

Modeling and Simulation

In writing on the importance of modeling and simulation in wargames and/or tabletop exercises and as replacements for case studies, I need to stress two points:

1. Modeling and simulation should take place throughout the program.
2. Warfighters/operators should participate throughout the program.

In Table 6-1, we see that these points are just as necessary (if not more so) in system integration. Manufacturing and developmental process outcomes can be gamed—especially when dealing with the inevitable potential for reconfiguration and/or a change in operational requirements. Simulations can optimize projected human interactions, information collection, artificial intelligence, and data analyses. Modeling and simulation across all systems integration processes provide the timely feedback and alternative approaches for informed decision making. The greater the integration, the greater and more dynamic are the ability and effectiveness of the decisions.

With regard to warfighter/operator involvement, we need only remember that Department of Defense (DoD) programs, especially those involving our nation's offensive and defensive weapons systems, leave the most compelling risks to in-theater operators, and not program managers. Warfighter/operators need to be involved in the system integration.

Personnel

System integration requires dedicated, focused, professionals with exceptional expertise. Excellent technology is not enough if the required integration expertise is not there to implement it. Organizations may struggle to find and retain employees with the required skill sets for system integration. Contractors may advertise having expertise even if it does not yet exist, hoping to pick it up on the fly. An external or "third-party" specialist/consultant may bring needed integration expertise to the table more expeditiously.

Technological "Yield" —Potential into Performance

Technological "yield" refers to how measurably successful the essential technologies are integrated into the overall product architecture, application and user environment. The yield, as described in performance metrics such as miles per hour, target acquisition range, or mean time between failures, is a measure of how close *actual* performance comes to *theoretical* performance. A high yield suggests a successful integration of the technology. That said, technological yield findings are not always immediate, accurate or predictive. Subsequent testing and re-testing may produce lower values, suggesting that the technology may not yet be mature and, therefore not ready for production and/or implementation.

System Integration Process

There is no such thing as a *standard* system integration. Every system uses different subsystems to achieve different goals. The System Integrator (or team) must understand all the current and predicted program requirements. Translating program requirements into needs, and continuously improving communication between program management and the system integration team, connect the visions of the designers with the program managers' realities.

Figure 6-2 describes how the system integration process fits in the big picture of program management. Again, nothing in the process is beyond the requirements of effective program management.

Figure 6-2. The System Integration Process

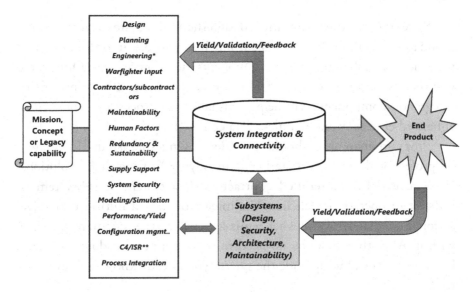

All applicable general and specialty engineering disciplines (including safety and environmental)

** Command, Control, Communications, Computers/Intelligence, Surveillance, and Reconnaissance

The task of integrating legacy or already existing subsystems into new systems or capabilities can require much research and effort. Only in recent years have systems been deployed that can interconnect innovative and existing subsystems. However, many systems and subsystems were "stovepipe" designs with no thought about future connectivity. Depending on their number and size, connecting several independent systems and subsystems into one while ensuring uninterrupted connectivity will take time and meticulousness. Successful system integration in the private sector helps forward-thinking companies to grow and prosper by automating many business processes and providing accurate decision-making data throughout.

The longest and the most challenging phase of the program can be where the actual integration is performed. Based on a logical architecture design, a physical equivalent is developed. If all previous steps have been followed with a close attention to detail, a system integrator should perform system integration successfully and easily, without losing valuable time, funding or data.

Design, Architecture and Maintainability

System integrators/teams must design the architecture to create strong foundations and to minimize risk as much as possible, in order to ensure that multiple subsystems and components function as one. Only then will the system meet (or exceed) mission requirements. Blueprints of the integration components will help to visualize the process(es). The goal is enhanced efficiency and seamless data connectivity.

Program managers should consider having subsystems integrated by professional integrators, rather than buying "off-the-shelf" solutions implemented by unqualified contractors. If a system or subsystem is difficult to operate or deficient, the integrator should initiate corrective action immediately. If and when a mission evolves, the system must evolve with it. Also, there may be no need to acquire a new product, as it can be more beneficial to upgrade the system you already know and find easy to use.

System Security

DoD programs (now and forever) will depend on the most accurate and actionable information, securely collected, stored and displayed. DoD security systems must protect data, information, and the knowledge acquired therefrom from theft, sabotage, accidents, misuse, and ignorance. The greater that amount of data—the greater the security challenge. The threat of cyber-attack will be with us always, and DoD programs must function in a cyber-secure environment—from preliminary design through the entire life cycle. Lives may depend on it.

How is information *networked*? The Internet may seem an obvious answer, but it is increasingly vulnerable to denial of service, hacking and physical destruction of the key "hubs" A dedicated military communication system is the default solution, although bandwidth allocation and management create additional challenges for program managers.

Organizational "Inertia" and Lack of Accountability

System integration always involves multiple players as well as multiple subsystems. Accountability for the success (or failure) of the integration becomes blurred very easily when integrating many different subsystems. There can be multiple stakeholders (e.g., vendors, users, system owners, etc.), none of them ultimately responsible for the entire system integration. Each may only handle or care at most about one piece of the integration and be unlikely to appreciate the big picture or have a sense of urgency for it. When something goes wrong, the situation turns almost immediately to finger pointing and blaming other parties instead of someone "owning" the integration. When a single party manages the system integration project, he or she is (often contractually) responsible and accountable for integration success, and there is no longer any ambiguity. Accountability replaces ambiguity.

Some decision makers elect to acquire new or off-the-shelf packages instead of integrating already existing subsystems. Contractors often procure only the components that they actually need at the moment or to solve an immediate problem. This way may be faster and cheaper in the beginning, and thus seem more profitable and efficient. But the practice can very quickly become counterproductive, as the new additions become obsolete or create interoperability problems down the road. As the program evolves, it may start using more and more independent, free-standing, tools, possibly resulting in productivity decline and inaccurate/inconsistent data analyses. The longer the project takes, the more significant this issue becomes. Records become confusing and incapable of audit. Funds are used faster or are prematurely exhausted. Problem correction is funded from other finding lines or kicked to the next fiscal year. Keeping the integration projects as short as possible can improve program success. Furthermore, an agile working methodology that can address changing requirements along the way and also after the project is essential for systems integration success.

The "good" news, remember, is that system integration *is* program management; and with DoD contracts, the program manager is in charge. He or she controls the funds, owns the integration and establishes subordinate responsibility and accountability accordingly. The challenge to program managers is the time-consuming and complicated nature of integrating various subsystems.

Problem-Solving and Continual Improvement

We cannot discuss day-in, day-out program management and system integration without discussing two indispensable "mindsets." A problem-solving mindset accepts the fact that problems are inevitable but that any problem can be corrected—and, if not corrected entirely, in some way mitigated. *"Don't fix the blame, fix the problem"* should be the reaction; appreciating that a problem, once identified, is half solved. International Quality Management Standards such as ISO 9001:2015 instruct that selected corrective actions should be realistic and measurable, and that follow-up must ensure that the corrective actions produced the desired results.

Closely related is the continual improvement mindset that reminds program managers that any system or process, however efficient, can always be made better. The program managers must always be on the lookout for opportunities to improve a system, process or situation. Outside auditors measure the continual improvement mindset in an organization by assessing:

- Adherence to policies and objectives
- Analysis of data and effectiveness or recurring reports
- Effectiveness of following up previous corrective and preventive actions
- Structured program reviews, with actionable findings, conclusions and recommendations.

Summary

There are essentially no more stand-alone operations or weapons. DoD programs, especially those involving our nation's offensive and defensive weapons systems, leave the most compelling risks and decisions to in-theater operators, not to stateside program managers or contractors. Connectivity in decision making means harnessing information from many information generators (or sensors) into one total picture.

Successful system integration and the need to streamline processes for more effective program management and warfighting is more important now than ever, due to the increasing advances in warfighting technology among major powers and the pernicious adventurism of a few thug nations.

Comprehensive program management creates, in its execution, successful system integration. Program managers need to stay focused on system integration throughout a program, and not as an end-of-pipe activity. Only then will integration of subsystems into a finalized system be possible.

CHAPTER SEVEN

System integration – Enabling Capability Through Connectivity

Part II Expeditionary Warfare and Battlespace Management

Recently, I attended a briefing by a major theater commander on the state of readiness of his area of responsibility. He used present - day terms like: *"Battlespace", "Expeditionary Warfare", "reach-back"*, and *"lethal weapons;"* but then sprinkled in discomforting, but not unfamiliar, expressions like *"fight with what you have", no space uncontested"*, and *"no safe havens".* Warfighters are living with these terms and expressions every day; program managers and contractors, however, may lose sight of them and may need to be reminded.

In the last chapter, I stressed the need to incorporate:

- Risk management and gap analysis;
- Operator/warfighter participation in program management;
- Meaningful feedback, follow-up, and accountability;
- Modeling and simulation, to include tabletop exercises and/or wargames; and
- Non-materiel solutions for materiel shortcomings.

> *Do everything you have to do – but do it faster!*

This chapter links System Integration and Program Management with Expeditionary Warfare and Battlespace Management. It is here where we emphasize the sense of urgency. Put another way: *Do everything you have to do — but do it faster.* As is often the case, the troops have been waiting too long already.

By way of review, System Integration is the process of bringing together the component sub-systems into one system. It is an aggregation of subsystems cooperating so that the resultant system is able to deliver an overarching functionality or capability, by ensuring that the subsystems function together as ONE system. In information technology, it is the process of linking together different computing systems and software applications physically or functionally, to act as a coordinated whole. An *integrated* system streamlines processes, reduces costs, and increases efficiency.

System Integration connects multiple discrete subsystems from different sources to work as one. Some subsystems are old, some are new. Program managers usually find that putting the subsystems together as early as possible in the program's development improves mission effectiveness and helps to ensure seamless *connectivity,* enabling commanders at the front and at the rear to better execute and evaluate strategic and tactical accomplishment.

Figure 7-1, partially from the last chapter, graphically displays System Integration as an essential subset of Program Management. It summarizes system integration well enough (I think), including the need for warfighter involvement. It goes on to show the linking of System Integration to the Battlespace. This direct and unimpeachable linking may be missing (and/or presumed lost) on contractors and program personnel.

Figure 7-1. The system integration process and the Battlespace

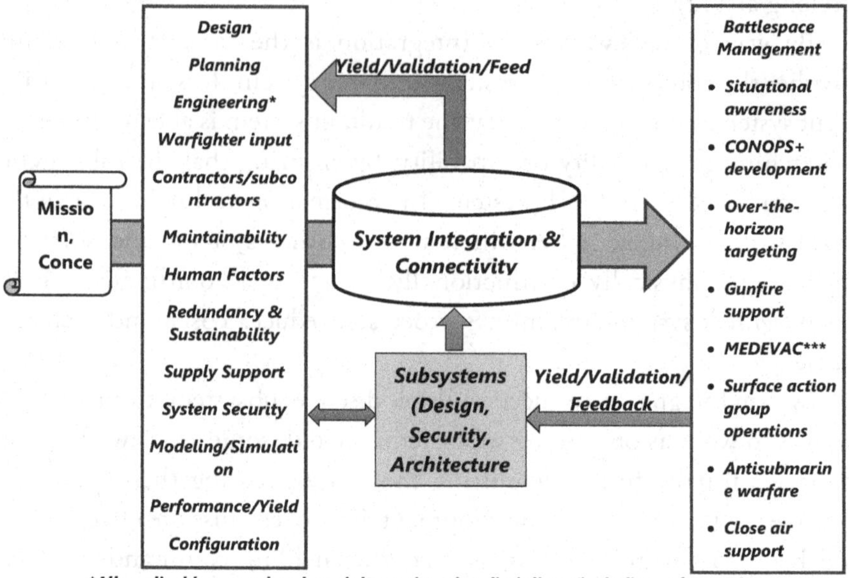

All applicable general and specialty engineering disciplines (including safety and environmental)

** Command, Control, Communications, Computers/Intelligence, Surveillance, and Reconnaissance*

Please note again in figure 1 the need for "Warfighter involvement," "technological yield," and "connectivity." They are essential, in the beginning and throughout a program's lifecycle. They are often neglected in a program's early stages, but are indispensable not only for managing the program, and for ensuring that subsystems and components successfully address the mission; and *integrate* those subsystems into a viable end product ("e.g.; a weapon system, with all hardware, software, training simulators, and logistic support).

Expeditionary Warfare and Battlespace Management

"Fight with what you have"
The unfortunate cliché becomes the unhappy battle cry.

Expeditionary warfare means deploying our fighting forces abroad, normally away from established bases. Historically, the U.S.'s ability to project its forces into distant areas has served as an effective diplomatic lever, influencing decision-making processes and acting as a potential deterrent on another states' inappropriate behavior or adventurism.

The aircraft carrier strike group, strategic bomber, ballistic missile submarine, and strategic airlifter are all examples of power projection platforms. Military units designed to be light and mobile, such as airborne forces (paratroopers and air assault forces) and amphibious assault forces, are utilized in power projection. Forward basing is another method of power projection, which, by pre-positioning military units or stockpiles of arms at strategically located military bases outside a country's territory, reduces the time and distance needed to mobilize them.

Expeditionary forces are the precursor of the rapid deployment forces. They must be (at least initially) self-sustaining, with a viable logistics support capability and with constant and undeviating stateside connectivity.

As the distance between a fighting force and its directing headquarters increases, command and control inevitably become more difficult. Modern-day power projection requires high-tech communications and information technology to succeed. Ships at sea in surface action groups (e.g.; an aircraft carrier and assigned cruisers and destroyers), capable of communicating with each other, must now coordinate with supplementing forces of other nations and with rear echelons. Missions, as well as forces, must be coordinated. Information, the one weapon that can be in more than one place at the same time, must be disseminated – rapidly and precisely. And you can't do that if communications systems are not totally integrated and uncompromisingly reliable.

Strategy in the briefing room becomes *tactics* at the front; and *"fight with what you have"* – the unfortunate cliché in the briefing room becomes the unhappy battle cry at the front.

Table 7-1, like figure 7-1, expands to include Expeditionary Warfare and Battlespace Management. The requirements are the same, and a shortcoming at the beginning carries through to the end.

Table 7-1 Comparing systems integration with program management, and then extending to Expeditionary Warfare and Battlespace Management

Requirement	Program Management	System Integration	Expeditionary Warfare	Battlespace Mgmt
Mission planning; concept development	✓	✓	✓	✓
Design/development (including hardware/software)	✓	✓	✓	✓
Modeling/Simulation	✓	✓	✓	✓
Research & development	✓	✓	✓	✓
Risk management plan	✓	✓	✓	✓
Gap analysis	✓	✓	✓	✓
Core team developed; responsibility/ accountability assigned (including decision makers)	✓	✓	✓	✓
Warfighter involvement	✓	✓	✓	✓
Performance-oriented; metrics developed/consistent/actionable	✓	✓	✓	✓
Test plans developed; tech yield identified	✓	✓	✓	✓
Contract in place; executable	✓	✓	✓	✓
Connectivity/feedback	✓	✓	✓	✓
Configuration/change management process defined/in place	✓	✓	✓	✓
Internal/external security procedures in place	✓	✓	✓	✓
Life cycle management plan	✓	✓	✓	✓

Having (notionally) brought operating forces into the theater, the next step is to organize, manage, and optimize operations in the Battlespace.

It's Show Time!

The military operational environment has transformed from primarily a time and space-driven, linear understanding (a "battlefield") to a multi-dimensional system of systems understanding (a battlespace) – a system of systems. Battlespaces are more complex, primarily because of the information age. Today, militaries are expected to understand the effects of their actions on the operational environment as a whole, and not just in the military domain of their operational environment.

Battlespace management describes a unified military strategy to integrate and combine expeditionary and allied armed forces in military theaters of operations; including land, air, sea, space, and cyberspace, to successfully apply combat power, protect the force, and complete the mission. Our warfighters must work *with* allied forces and often *within* different chains of command and spans of control. Artillery fire, Naval gunfire, and close air support, (e.g.; during amphibious landings), often delineated with imaginary boundary lines, challenge compatibility and connectivity. Similar goals and objectives must be achieved using dissimilar forces and resources.

Superiority in the Battlespace also means that the *speed* at which the warfighting organization develops and transforms knowledge into actions for desired effects in the battlespace must be faster than the opposition at doing the right actions at the right time and place.

Battlespace agility is dependent on the quality of situational awareness and holistic understanding of the battlespace, in order to determine the best actions – a logic that has become a driving force behind a renaissance of interest in the quality of military intelligence. It is also about executing the most effective actions in the most efficient manner relative to achieving the desired impact.

Worth remembering is that if a weapons system or platform has reached the battlespace, it had better reflect the absolute best tenets and efforts of DoD program management. It may be impossible to fix a problem in theater, with any degree of timeliness.

Once the system or platform is in theater, reach-back support must be structured, streamlined, and responsive, to ensure optimum performance. Unfortunately, even in the cyber-age, connectivity between key nodes of the supply chain stateside and the warfighters in the Battlespace continues to be sluggish, erratic, and bordering on dysfunctional. This after over eighteen years in Afghanistan and twice that long in the Middle East.

Again, the Theater Commander in his briefing used the terms: *"No safe havens," "no uncontested spaces"* and *"lethal weapons."* DoD has serious limits on where, how much, and how often it can *exercise* forces in advance of actual operations. And we need to consider all weapons as lethal. Therefore, training exercises, especially in advance of a unit's deployment, must be up-to-date, and as realistic as possible, consistent with safety. Lessons learned from the exercises must be comprehensive and meaningful – with maximum dissemination and with realistic, measurable, corrective action plans.

Weapons systems and platforms (e.g.; HUMVEEs), once in the Battlespace, must have all compatibility issues resolved; and range and depth of replacement parts must be equal to the demand. Quantities of consumables (e.g.; gas masks and cannisters) must reflect normal and surge requirements, and be subject to periodic review and verification.

Tactical decisions in support of battlespace management (e.g.; in a surface action group) must address all of the above, under fluctuating conditions of infrastructure, weather, terrain, and the electromagnetic spectrum; and reflect threat assessments, intelligence, and situational awareness within the operational areas and areas of focus.

Optimally, *in-theater* tactical decisions should reflect pre-deployment fleet and/or logistics exercises, wargames, and tried and true concepts of operations, using tried and true weapons and platforms, in accordance with well-developed concepts of operations (CONOPS). This may no longer be possible, as we run out of both time, space, and opportunity to practice core competencies. And there never seems to be sufficient funding to support meaningful training. Funding for mission essentials such as training schools, software, and simulators, which should be fenced, is often expended during the building phase to solve a problem, and no longer available when needed.

Deploying units replacing their counterparts in-theater require a comprehensive pre-deployment turnover strategy, one that reflects months of connectivity and interaction before the actual turnover takes place.

SUMMARY

System Integration is an indispensable subset of Program Management. Programs become products, and products find their way to the Battlespace. They must perform as required (and sustainably) in the Battlespace; U.S. lives and missions may depend on it. If that product, be it a weapons system, platform, or a piece of communication equipment, fails – somebody may not make it home.

If a weapon system or platform has reached the battlespace, it had better reflect the absolute best doctrines and efforts of proactive DoD program management.

"Fight with what you have," the unfortunate cliché in the briefing room remains the unhappy battle cry at the front.

Program managers and contractors must recognize and support what warfighters already know all too well, that:

- Weapon systems or platforms have vital end uses in support of mission commitments;
- Successful end use requires urgency of arrival in-theater, and sustainability of operations in-theater;
- U.S. lives and U.S. missions depend on those weapons systems and platforms; and
- Rapid deployment does not mean rapid conclusion. There are currently no short-term involvements and there are not likely to be any. Eighteen-plus years in Afghanistan proves that. Please see my article on Afghanistan Reconstruction in the January – February 2020 issue of *Defense Acquisition*.

I have spent over 50 years in direct or indirect support of the Department of Defense. If one of my programs showed signs of failure and I did not act, I would rather have faced one dozen unhappy flag officers in the Pentagon than one unprotected 19-year-old service member at the front.

CHAPTER EIGHT

Simulations Versus Case Studies in Decision-Making

Not "What Happened?" but "What If?" What's Next?" and (Hopefully) "What a Good Idea!"

In the Navy, we used to say that there are three types of officers: those who *make* things happen, those who *watch* things happen and those who say: *"What happened?"*.

We can no longer afford "Number 3." We must support those who make things happen and give the right analytical tools to those assigned to watch things happen; so that everybody knows "What happened?"

Last year, I wrote an article for *Defense AT&L* titled *"Tabletop Exercises—An Affordable 'Value-Add' in the Acquisition Process* in which I recommended using tabletop exercises when wargames are too hard to develop, fund or schedule. In this article, I suggest not only that the tabletop is superior to the case study, but that, by applying basic risk, probability and gaming simulation, developers can create a meaningful tabletop *or* wargame where only a case study previously existed. Unlike the *here it is, read it* structure of the case study, tabletops and wargames are *iterative* processes, wherein the players work through timely scenarios. The dynamic structure of the simulations helps the players not only to arrive at (hopefully correct) decisions, but to work through decision processes and learn about the effects of those decisions.

Unlike standalone case studies, simulations *come to life*, by providing:

- An actual, iterative sequence of events
- Player participation in the play of the game
- Immediate (albeit artificial) feedback
- Critical analyses, versus simple data review
- New theories for testing—and their implications
- An early appreciation for the *fog of war*.

Since our college days at least, we have worked with case studies. What Business Administration student could ever forget the *Acme Widget Company*? Case studies were a great way for inexperienced kids in classrooms to stretch their new brain muscles around problems long past but often repeated. These days, there is only limited value to gaining proficiency with what already happened. We need to go further. Certainly, we need to learn from the past, but we need to take away what is important and apply it optimally to challenges yet to come—and do so quickly.

DoD should take whatever worthwhile case study and history data it can extract from the past and use it to *inform and predict* the future— discarding what it doesn't need and *modeling* the rest to enhance what it does need.

Defining Terms

A *case study* is a process or record of research in which detailed consideration is given to developing a particular person, group or situation over a period of time—or a particular instance of something used or analyzed in order to illustrate a thesis or principle. The problem with case studies is that often they (at best) stop short of providing a productive mental exercise, or (at worst) leave users with unproven and likely erroneous root causes and conclusions—already arrived at. Data collected from case studies can provide a starting place and (perhaps) a working hypothesis for simulations, and, possibly tabletops and wargames.

A *simulation* is an imitation of a situation or process, or the action of pretending; deception, or the production of a computer model of something, especially for the purpose of study, analysis and prediction.

Many of the criticisms directed at military simulations result from an incorrect application of them as a predictive and analytical tool. Basic simulations tend to produce three sets of results: a best, intermediate, and worst-case outcome. It is not my intention here to bury the reader in algorithms and formulae, linear programming, Monte Carlo, or the theory of games. The best approach is the one that gets actionable answers without scaring away the participants. We'll stay at a 50,000 feet elevation for now.

Outcomes supplied by models rely on human interpretation and therefore should not be regarded as providing "gospel truth."

In a *tabletop exercise* key personnel who are assigned high level roles and responsibilities are brought together to deliberate various simulated emergency or rapid response situations. Tabletop exercises (conducted in conference rooms) are often the first opportunity that participants from different commands have to meet and gain appreciation for each other's capabilities and shortcomings.

A *wargame* is a type of warfare modeling, including simulation, campaign and systems analysis, and military exercises; and a simulated battle or campaign to test military concepts and uses. Wargames normally are conducted in dedicated facilities with officers acting as opposing staffs; and with actual force members participating. And the games are refereed by umpires.

> **Analyze the past and predict the future—**
> **or else don't waste your time.**

Each of the four activities as defined has, to varying degrees: objectives, a scenario, and data. That much is basic, and you need it to be informed. However, to analyze and predict, you also need models, rules, and players. And analysts. Like umpires, analysts are vital. Analyze the past and predict the future—or else don't waste your time.

Figure 8-1 describes where the case study fits in dynamic, predictive modeling and simulation. It reminds the reader that the case study, however informative, is a "done deal" unless and until it becomes part of a greater enterprise.

Figure 8-1. Using case studies in simulation decision making

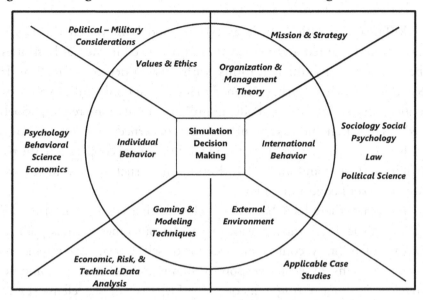

Figure 8-2 describes the dynamic nature of a process worthy of the time spent on it. A *case study* would appear in the "Research" bubble as essentially a finished product—informative but inert. *Simulation* begins in the Integration bubble. The constant churning of ideas (clockwise arrows) and feedback (counterclockwise arrows) takes developers well past case studies and into tabletops or wargames.

Figure 8-2. Developing a tabletop or wargame

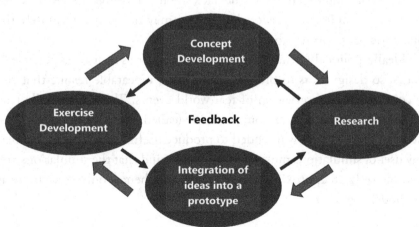

Political-Military simulations (exciting stuff)

Military simulations (wargames) are models in which theories of warfare can be tested and refined without the need for actual hostilities. They exist in many different forms, with varying degrees of realism. In recent times, their scope has widened to include not only military but also political and social factors. Political-military simulations remain widely used today. Often, modern simulations are concerned not with a potential war between superpowers but more with international cooperation, the rise of global terrorism and smaller brushfire conflicts such as those in Kosovo, Bosnia, Sierra Leone and Sudan.

For years, there have been many charges that computerized models are unrealistic and slanted toward particular outcomes. Critics point to the case of military contractors seeking to sell a weapons system. For obvious reasons of cost, weapons systems are extensively computer modeled. Without testing of its own, the Department of Defense (DoD) may need to rely largely on the manufacturer's own models configured to show weapons systems under ideal conditions, with actual operational effectiveness turning out to be less than stated.

Human error is another factor that can render a model/simulation invalid. A programming error (a guided missile cruiser consistently steaming at 70 knots) can produce outrageously incorrect outcomes. Human factors, such as training, expertise, and morale frequently lead to programming snags and complications.

Available intelligence (or the lack thereof) brings its own set of snags and complications. Modelers simply may not know accurately the capabilities or opposing forces.

Ideally, political-military simulations should be as realistic as possible—that is, so designed as to provide measurable, repeatable results that can be confirmed by observation of real-world events. This is especially true for simulations that are random in nature (called "stochastic"), as they are used in a manner that is intended to produce useful, predictive outcomes. Any user of simulations must always bear in mind that the simulations are, however, only an approximation of reality and, hence, only as accurate as the model itself.

Disaster preparedness simulation can replicate emergency situations, train first responders, and develop concepts of operation. Disaster preparedness simulation can involve training on how to handle terrorist attacks, natural disasters such as hurricanes, pandemic outbreaks, or other life-threatening emergencies.

Management simulations

Even short of simulating combat situations, (i.e., in actual tabletops and wargames) simulation has contributions to offer In Finance, Project Management, Training, Risk Analysis and Management, Needs Analysis, Supply Chain Management, and general decision-making. Basically, any tasks requiring:

- Evaluation of strategies and core values
- Life-cycle product or system management
- Identification and evaluation of alternative approaches
- Analysis and quantification of strategies, goals and objectives
- Database development and data analysis
- Identifying potential synergies and innovations
- Metrics and measures of effectiveness
- Assignment responsibilities
- Performance-based contract administration
- Actionable courses of corrective action.

Project management simulation, for example is often used for present and future project managers in the private sector. In some cases, simulations are used for "what-if" analyses and for supporting decision making in real projects. The simulation often is conducted using specific software. It also often is used to analyze and evaluate planned and existing projects. The goal of the simulation is to show the user the different possible outcomes of his or her decisions, along with the probability of each outcome. Simulation helps in reducing the project risk and in choosing the optimal approach. In a typical simulation, the project is first modeled with a software tool and use of uncertain variables. A simulation then is run to check the different possible outcomes and their probability as a result of different inputs for the uncertain variables.

The use of simulation throughout a product's life cycle, especially at the earlier concept and design stages, offers possible benefits, ranging from direct cost reductions as in reduced prototyping and shorter time to service use and better performing products with longer service lives.

Continuous improvement

Every modern management program, regardless of purpose or focus, must be executed with a continuous improvement mindset; and simulations provide managers with sneak peeks into continuous improvement innovations and opportunities. If a model does not add value and include continuous improvement, it's not ready for use.

Unlike when dealing with opposing forces, modelers of management-related simulations will likely possess robust data and a high degree of situational awareness—making their validity and contribution greater.

Validation

In the development of simulations, *validation* is the process of testing a model by supplying it with historical data and comparing its output with the known historical result. If a model can reliably reproduce known results, it is considered to be validated and assumed to be capable of providing predictive outputs within a reasonable degree of uncertainty.

Progressively gaining robustness, payback, and "value add"

The payback from each of the four approaches described (case study, simulation, tabletop, and wargame), like the approaches themselves, directly reflects the level of preparation and execution. Figure 8-3 and Table 1 demonstrate how progressing from standalone case studies, through wargames by the accelerated employment of simulation, takes developers from information of the past to prediction of the future, with attendant increases in utility, comprehensiveness and realism.

Figure 8-3 Progressively gaining robustness, payback, and "value-add" through simulation

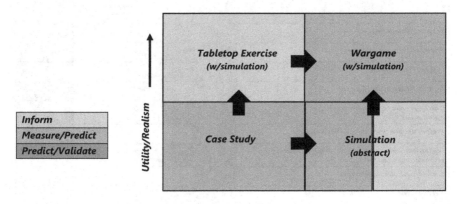

Planners and project managers need more than historic information and anecdotal evidence. They need the capability to subject that information to critical analysis, while all the time honing their own analytical skills and professional competence. They need to develop actionable findings and predictions, and to validate them.

Table 8-1, in applying Figure 8-3, describes how developers can predict and validate their concepts by increasing the robustness of the effort.

Table 8-1. Specific areas for improvement through simulation

Areas for Improvement	Case Study	Simulation/ Modeling	Tabletop*	Wargame*
Program Management	■	■		■
Strategy/Concept development	■	■		■
Disaster Preparedness	■	■		■
Doctrine/checklist development	■	■		■
Develop/model performance metrics/measures of effectiveness	■	■		■
Pre/post incident evaluation & "hot washup"	■			■
Conclusions, action plans, milestones, assignment of responsibilities, and feedback	■	■		■
Computer-modeled simulations	■			■
Needs assessment	■	■		■
Threat/Risk assessment	■			■
Connectivity, Command and Control	■	■		■
Decision development	■	■		■
Preliminary validation of operations and tactics	■	■		■
Actual elements of Armed Forces participating	■	■		■
Two-sided, opposing, umpired maneuver	■	■		■

Start with the column marked "Areas for Improvement" which lists the focus areas (feel free to put in your own). Then:

- Apply mission-centric goals and objectives
- Gather available, *useful* data
- Determine what needs to be verified and validated, looking always for areas of potential synergy and innovation
- Consider the entire life cycle of involved systems and equipment, including training simulators
- Develop tentative conclusions for testing.

And then:

- Develop models and simulations
- Work them in realistic scenarios with all positions filled by experts
- Develop and/or identify decision points

- Identify actionable intelligence for realistic prediction and decision making
- Develop feedback loops.

You have now developed the foundation for (at least) a comprehensive tabletop or (at best) a comprehensive wargame.

Summary

Decision making in DoD requires simulations, tabletops, and wargames; they must be structured to allow players to make decisions and to measure and predict the impacts of those decisions. DoD needs to embrace simulation not only for realistic warfare planning and training but for responsive project management.

In the classroom, simulations can become a "living" textbook addressing challenges in the present and creating/recreating the curriculum of the future and a vital and indispensable part of the DoD acquisition processes. In the game room, simulations scrutinize ideas and theories, assessing and predicting outcomes with minimal time and funding requirements with the goals of preserving life and fulfilling the mission.

CHAPTER NINE

Program Management Mindsets –Success Through Focus

In decision theory and in general systems theory, a *mindset* is a set of assumptions, methods, or notions held by one or more people or groups of people. A mindset can also be seen as arising out of a person's worldview or philosophy of life.

A mindset may be so firmly established that it creates a powerful incentive within people or groups to continue adopting or accepting prior behaviors, choices, or tools. The latter phenomenon also is sometimes described as *mental inertia*, or *groupthink*, and it is often difficult to counteract its effects upon analyses and decision-making processes.

There are two different types of mindsets: (1) Fixed mindset: Situations are inborn, fixed, and unchangeable. *"We've always done it that way"* and (2) Growth mindset: Situations can be developed and strengthened, by focus, commitment, and hard work. *"Why do we always do it that way?"*

In a fixed mindset, individuals working in program management may believe that their basic abilities, intelligence, and talents, are just fixed traits. They have a certain amount and that's that, and then their goal becomes to look smart all the time and never look dumb.

In a *growth* mindset, success-oriented individuals understand that their programs can be enhanced through effort, good management practices, and perseverance. They don't necessarily believe that they can achieve perfection, but they do believe that their programs can always be made better, more robust, and more defensible if they work at it. Individuals with growth mindsets are more likely to continue working hard despite setbacks.

The sections that follow describe growth mindsets that I have observed and written about many times over the years. The first is the cornerstone mindset for successful program management: Continuous Improvement.

> *A Mindset is a continuing focus on the big picture, reminding the manager that something can always be made better.*

1. Continuous improvement

A continuous improvement process, often called a *continual* improvement process, is an ongoing effort to improve products, services, or processes. Continuous improvement seeks "incremental" improvement over time, and sometimes, "breakthrough" improvement all at once. Figure 9-1 summarizes the continuous improvement mindset in action.

Figure 9-1. The Continuous Improvement Mindset

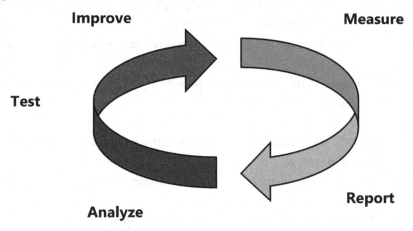

Continuous improvement cycle means that you:

1. Analyze the target process.
2. Test the process(es); establish desired performance goals.
3. Develop measurable improvements.
4. Measure the improved process; develop an action plan to achieve the goals.
5. Report findings; establish ongoing feedback.

Note Step 5: If you don't have feedback, you will never be certain of the success (or failure) of the other steps.

2. Corporate responsibility management

DoD program managers and DoD contractors need to identify all the ethical issues associated with contract performance. The contractors need to recognize their obligation to deliver value and the direct relationship between their reputation and that value. Contractors put their names on their product, whether they realize it or not; and DoD validates their performance, whether it realizes that or not. Day-in/day-out allegiance to a corporate responsibility management system starts at the top—by example and not by fiat.

Organizational *ethics* concerns systemic reflection on the rules and issues of the ways in which people act. A robust corporate responsibility management program institutionalizes those ethical rules and practices in the conduct of the organization. For our purposes, corporate responsibility management is the creation and control of processes by which DoD contractors perform to established, measurable, standards of ethical practice.

A DoD contractor's corporate responsibility management policy and program development should:

- ✓ Clearly state management's commitment to high standards of ethical practice.
- ✓ Be consistent with management's vision and strategies for the future.
- ✓ Permit measurable objectives to be developed.
- ✓ Be widely disseminated within the organization and among other stakeholders.
- ✓ Document its objectives clearly and be reviewed routinely, and be the object of continual improvement.
- ✓ Be reflected in all material written and produced.

3. Risk assessment and management

Terms like *risk analysis, risk assessment,* and *risk management* often are used interchangeably and can include various different concepts or strategies. Approaches can be simple or complex, although simpler is almost always better. Properly conducted risk management permits decision making based on realistic scenario assumptions and provides defensible justification, before limited resources are committed.

Properly conducted risk assessments based on lifelike scenario assumptions lead program managers to either justify or preclude commitments of time and funding in making their decisions.

There are many approaches to meaningful risk management. Modeling (e.g., using an EXCEL Spreadsheet) provides risk planners with a simple but comprehensive management tool for identifying mission threats, criticalities and vulnerabilities. Best of all, it can help identify and assess logical, defensible, conclusions and potentially mitigating actions.

4. Quality management

> *If the product or service does not meet the specifications, some of the customers or end users may not come home.*

In my 50+ years of management experience, I know of few expressions more used, abused, or otherwise amateurishly bantered around more than "quality." The "cop-out" definition of quality used to be "conformance to specifications." That would bring the hit-the-wall response: *"So, then, is a Ford Pinto built to specifications of higher quality than a Rolls-Royce that may not be?"* Such is the stuff of broke companies and rich consultants. You need not worry about it.

You *do* need to worry about the thornier follow-on definition: "Meets or exceeds the requirements of the customer." That begs the question: *"Who is the customer, and (therefore) who defines Quality?"* That's easy, Mr./Ms. DoD program manager: You are and you do. You and the contractor must develop a robust quality management plan for the product or service, complete with milestones, metrics, audits, feedback loops, and reviews; and you must totally involve the warfighters.

Management focuses on audit results and milestone achievement; mindset also focuses on mission fulfillment (of the product or service), and the scrupulous involvement and feedback of warfighters. Warfighters are nearly always the customer or the end user. If the product or service does not meet the specifications, some of them really may not come home. Remember that.

5. Sustainment

For DoD, sustainment is the provision of logistics, financial management, personnel services, and health service support necessary to maintain operations until successful mission completion. Sustainment operations enable force readiness.

A sustainment mindset means the ability to foresee operational requirements and initiate actions that satisfy a response without waiting for an operation order or fragmentary order. Forward-thinking sustainment commanders and staffs *visualize* future operations, identify required support, and start the processes of acquiring and providing the sustainment that best supports the operation. Tabletop exercises are an excellent venue for such visualization.

Sustainment planners should anticipate requirements before maneuver task force commanders ask for them, and posture vehicles and drivers ahead of time.

Continuity means providing uninterrupted sustainment across all levels of war. It is achieved through a system of integrated and focused networks that link sustainment to support capabilities and operations across all levels of war. Continuity ensures confidence in sustainment, which allows commanders freedom of action, increased operational reach, and prolonged endurance.

6. Environmental management

> *If you think that having an environmental management program is expensive, try not having one.*

Technically complex environmental problems seem to outnumber simple, effective mitigations. This leads to public confusion, frustration, discouragement, and (eventually) apathy. However, if you think having an environmental management program is expensive, try *not* having one. Let that sink in. I have given that warning to many clients. Most listened, but some didn't; and the most necessary DoD program can be stopped dead in its tracks if a DoD contractor (a shipyard, for example) creates an environmentally hazardous incident.

However laudable or necessary your program, your contactor will not succeed without a proactive environmental management program, one with strong roots in pollution prevention and energy conservation. It is not enough that a DoD contractor be environmentally *compliant.* Environmental *compliance* is not environmental *management.* Your contractors are not in charge when they are only in compliance. Only when they have effective environmental management programs are they not only compliant, but ethical, responsible, profitable, self-sustaining, and the best neighbor possible.

An environmental management mindset constantly reminds contractors and program managers that:

- Environmental strategies complement each other. Reducing pollutant generated reduces the complexity of the recycling or disposal effort. Also, conserving energy reduces pollution (e.g., less exhaust gas).

- Environmental strategies produce opportunities for cost avoidance. For example, initiatives such as "going paperless" or recycling office paper reduces not only waste, but the cost of disposing of it. Conserving energy lowers operating costs.

- Effective pollution prevention begins with realizing that there is no one all-encompassing solution to environmental problems. Rather, we need to identify all the problems, and then identify a broad spectrum of preventive and corrective measures, looking always for "synergies" whereby one action solves or mitigates more than one problem.

- Effective pollution prevention can mean technologically improving a process, or just not doing it at all. Simply reducing the number of times that you do something (or by not doing it anymore) does not require a big research and development budget. And it will make a measurable improvement almost immediately.

- Physical waste is not only an environmental problem that must be dealt with; it is a waste of an organization's time and resources. Recycling pollutant material is good, but not as good as not creating it in the first place.

7. Test planning

Test planning consists primarily of (1) development testing during the component design process, and (2) unit qualification testing to ensure that the final production design meets specifications. Component test plans may create attendant requirements for design of the test equipment itself, plus allocation of required support funding.

A test planning mindset means that program managers should identify every point in which a component or system requires testing and validation, the degree of accuracy, and the data to be collected and analyzed. Where management focuses on the test planning, mindset focuses on that plus the feedback from the testing and how it is re-incorporated into the component, the system, the final product, and the mission for which it was created.

8. Cyber security

Cyber security, also referred to as "information technology security," focuses on protecting computers, networks, programs and data from unintended or unauthorized access, change or destruction.

Governments, military, corporations, financial institutions, hospitals and other businesses collect, process and store a great deal of confidential information on computers and transmit that data across networks to other computers. With the growing volume and sophistication of cyber-attacks, ongoing attention is required to protect sensitive business and personal information, as well as safeguard national security.

A cyber-security mindset means that program managers must be security managers as well; make security one of their missions, and then approach it like any other. They just establish policies and procedures, conduct risk assessments, implement processes, identify corrective actions. And audit.

9. Reliability-centered maintenance

Reliability-centered maintenance (RCM) focuses on ensuring that equipment always functions reliably. RCM involves assessing each piece of equipment (or component) individually and as part of a larger system and in terms of how it is being used, or in some quantifiable measurement scheme. RCM identifies weak or failure points and uses that information to develop systems and schedules of *preventive* maintenance.

Comprehensive preventive maintenance programs for systems or equipment will, in turn, impact personnel manning, training and / or qualification requirements, maintenance down times, simulators, and stock inventory and / or turnover.

An RCM mindset requires continuously examining and addressing actual and potential reliability issues and failures, and revising maintenance requirements as appropriate.

10. System integration and connectivity

System Integration involves bringing together component subsystems into one system. It is an aggregation of subsystems cooperating so that the resultant system is able to deliver an overarching functionality or capability, by ensuring that the subsystems function together as *one* system. In information technology, it is the process of linking together different computing systems and software applications, physically or functionally, to act as a coordinated whole. An integrated system streamlines processes, reduces costs, and increases efficiency.

System Integration, as described in figure 9-2, connects multiple separate components which often come from different sources to work as one. Some subsystems are old, some are new. Program managers usually find that putting the subsystems together as early as possible in the program's development improves mission effectiveness and helps to ensure seamless *connectivity,* enabling commanders at the front and at the rear to better execute and assess strategic and tactical accomplishment.

Figure 9-2. System Integration and Connectivity

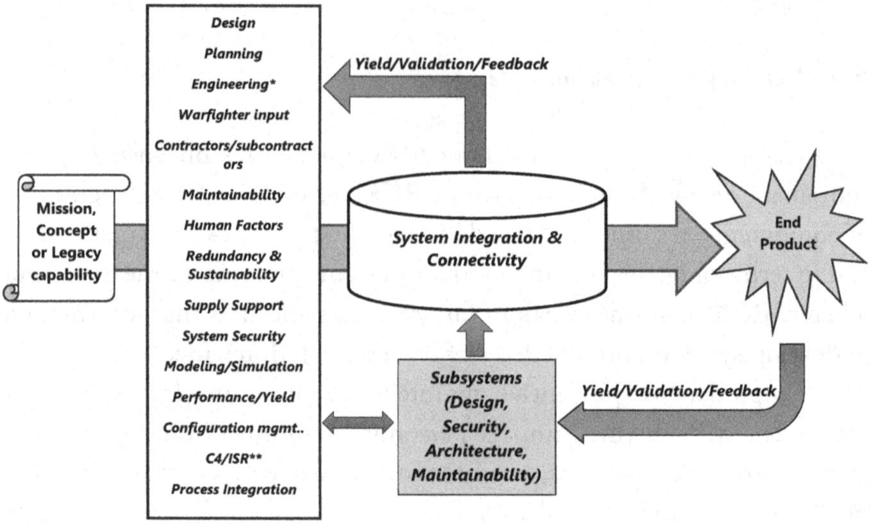

Design
Planning
Engineering*
Warfighter input
Contractors/subcontractors
Maintainability
Human Factors
Redundancy & Sustainability
Supply Support
System Security
Modeling/Simulation
Performance/Yield
Configuration mgmt..
C4/ISR**
Process Integration

Mission, Concept or Legacy capability

System Integration & Connectivity

Yield/Validation/Feedback

End Product

Subsystems (Design, Security, Architecture, Maintainability)

Yield/Validation/Feedback

*All applicable general and specialty engineering disciplines (including safety and environmental)

** Command, Control, Communications, Computers/Intelligence, Surveillance, and Reconnaissance

Connectivity refers to a program's or device's ability to link with other programs or devices. For example, a program that can import data from a wide variety of sources and can export data in many different formats is said to have "good connectivity," especially when connecting to or communicating with another computer or computer system.

Summary

A mindset is a matter of maintaining continued focus on the big picture, reminding program managers that something can always be made better.

Mindset means that a DoD contractor's responsibility to his employees and suppliers goes beyond writing checks. The contractor has an obligation to be fair and honest and a right to expect the same in return. Quality management was likely the first official home of the "mindset," and has been since before the earliest writings of Fredrick W. Taylor. The mindset constantly ponders "How do we make it better? How do we make it faster, or get it to the front faster? How do we make more of them for the same cost?"

The finest subsystems are useless (or at least fall short) if they cannot effectively connect with each other and form the system. Connectivity in decision making means harnessing information from many information generators (or sensors) into one total picture—often called the *Commander's Dashboard.*

This is not the time to worry about "global warming" and "climate change." DoD program managers and contractors must base environmental management strategy on pollution prevention and energy conservation; and make real, quantifiable, improvements to real, quantifiable, problems. If we all do our best to minimize pollution and conserve energy, the polar bears will be just fine, thank you. Table 9-1 describes mindset development and operation in action. Note the reference to applicable International Standards Organization (ISO) management standards. Ideally, contractors should *certify* to those standards. However, downloading them will provide immediate guidance, understanding, and direction to even the most over-worked program manager.

Table 9-1. Mindset in Action

Nr.	Mindset	Mindset in Action (DoD and Contractor)	Plus Regular Auditing	Applicable ISO Standard	Measure of Effectiveness
1	Continuous Improvement	Program reviews; trend/gap analyses; operator feedback; Customer complaint analyses	YES	All	Availability vs. Downtime Mission effectiveness
2	Corporate Responsibility Mgmt	Code of Ethics & Standards of Conduct Issue Identification & corrective action	YES	9000	Productivity; morale Contract Execution
3	Risk Assessment and Mgmt	Ongoing threat analyses/revision; Course of action (COA) development	YES	9000	COA Feedback
4	Quality Mgmt	Program reviews; trend/gap analyses; operator feedback; Customer complaints	YES	9000	Waste reduction Increased units\hour Increased early\on-time delivery

5	Sustainment	Future operations sustainment planning	YES	28000	Supply chain responsiveness Mission completion
6	Environmental management	Ongoing pollution prevention/energy conservation initiatives Material substitutions; process improvement	YES	14000	Physical waste reduction (tons/gallons)
7	Test Planning	Test and Evaluation Master Plan review/improvement	YES	9000	Mission Effectiveness
8	Cybersecurity	Firewall development/enhancement Penetration testing	YES	27000	Mission security
9	Reliability-centered Maintenance	Preventive maintenance plan development/revision Ongoing process review/improvement	YES	9000	Availability vs. Downtime FMEA**
10	System Integration and connectivity	Process improvement/streamlining Increased connectivity	YES	27000	Mission effectiveness

ISO 9000: Quality Mgmt; ISO 14000: Environment Mgmt; ISO 27000 Information Systems Mgmt; ISO 28000: Supply Chain Security

**Failure mode and effects analysis*

CHAPTER TEN

Collecting Lessons Learned

The Good, the Bad, and the Ugly—and Learning Something from Each

> *Nothing is more cost-effective than getting everything*
> *you can out of the funds you already have spent.*

Nothing is more cost-effective than getting everything you can out of the funds you already have spent. Let that sink in. Your program's funding already is identified, obligated, and being spent. You will get a product at the end. But will it be worth what you spent—or could you have built it cheaper, better, or faster?

Don't wait too late to find those answers, or to identify a nonconforming product or service that could have been corrected during development or manufacture. When the project is done, you may have no choice but to back-fit or modify- or throw it away entirely. Collecting lessons learned is too important to be left until the end. By then it is too late for that program and probably for your next one as well.

Some years ago, I was one of a team of subject-matter experts commissioned to analyze maritime operations during Operation Iraqi Freedom. The operation had been completed by then, and our sponsor told us to *"report what we did right."* No lessons-learned data had been corrected until then. We were forced to reconstruct tracks, sift through thousands of e-mails—barely 10 percent of which were relevant—and interview mariners long after their reassignment. Worst of all, no input had ever been solicited from the Warfighters, many of whom jumped at our invitation to participate in the analysis.

In the end, we analyzed what we wanted, interviewed whom we wanted, and created our own set of questions and metrics. We reported the "Good," and there was plenty of it. However, we also reported what was "Bad" and what was "Ugly." It is good to be the subject-matter expert.

Lessons learned are findings and experiences distilled from a project, lessons that should be actively taken into account not only in future projects, but for "mid-course corrections" to current projects. Findings may be positive, as in a successful test or mission—or negative, as in a mishap or failure.

The two most serious mistakes that a program manager can make to render lessons learned ineffective (read: meaningless) are (1) to not include *warfighter/user* input; and (2) to wait until the end of the program to collect them.

Regrettably, capturing lessons learned is usually thought of as a standalone, static, act —awaiting conclusion of the program or exercise. Furthermore, the end-product, once collected, often enjoys a late launching, a limited distribution, and (worst of all) a lack of distribution to participants whose contribution would likely be uncomplimentary or disapproving.

A dynamic and ongoing strategy of collecting lessons learned in real time is vastly more meaningful than collecting them at the end of the effort. Collecting lessons learned after the fact, and with all the damage done, is more correctly called an *investigation*. Nobody likes investigations.

It can be difficult to keep track of lessons learned in a timely manner without a formalized strategy. Learning a lesson about a program has, assuredly, the potential to improve the next program. Equally important, however, is the potential for an existing program it improve itself.

A robust and ongoing program of capturing lessons learned is essential to dealing with (but not limited to):

- Risk identification and prioritization
- Best practices
- Design issues
- Test planning and revision
- Budget and quality plans

- Delivery schedules
- Manpower and training requirements.

Risk identification and prioritization form the basis for developing, validating, or revising best (management) practices. Design issues can come from the factory floor, the battlespace, or any place in-between.

Figure 10-1 describes an ongoing approach to capturing lessons learned in a timely manner.

Figure 10-1. An Ongoing Approach to Capturing Lessons Learned

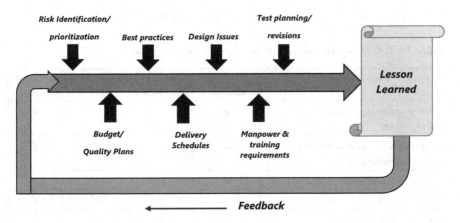

Again, effective, actionable, lessons learned must be captured and analyzed in real time, with corrective actions initiated as soon as possible. They cannot be exclusively the subject of after-action reports or "hot wash-ups." Find the problem, apply an appropriate corrective action— and then follow up to assess the effectiveness of the corrective action. Meaningful after-action reports (by whatever title) will state the findings, but should also state the corrections, and the (measurable) effectiveness of those corrections.

Start With the Project Plan—Everything for Lessons Learned

You need to have at your disposal: the program goals and objectives; metrics; feedback loops/status reports; and user/Warfighter input. Get all the input as soon as possible—go over everything, and remember that gathering lessons learned is a continuous process.

Start collecting data at the beginning and keep collecting throughout the program—don't wait until the end and try to reconstruct. Problem areas need to be addressed immediately. Eagles recognize that—ostriches don't.

Table 10-1 is taken from a previous article of mine applying program management requirements first to System Integration, and then to Expeditionary Warfare and Battlespace Management. Those same requirements appear again in Table 3. The requirements are generic, and the reader is welcome to substitute as appropriate.

Table 10-1. Getting the Material for the Lessons Learned

Requirement	Program Management	System Integration	Expeditionary Warfare	Battlespace Mgmt
Mission planning; concept development	✓	✓	✓	✓
Design/development (including hardware/software)	✓	✓	✓	✓
Modeling/Simulation	✓	✓	✓	✓
Research & development	✓	✓	✓	✓
Risk management plan	✓	✓	✓	✓
Gap analysis	✓	✓	✓	✓
Core team developed; responsibility/ accountability assigned (including decision makers)	✓	✓	✓	✓
Warfighter involvement	✓	✓	✓	✓
Performance-oriented; metrics developed/consistent/actionable	✓	✓	✓	✓
Test plans developed; tech yield identified	✓	✓	✓	✓
Contract in place; executable	✓	✓	✓	✓
Connectivity/feedback	✓	✓	✓	✓
Configuration/change management process defined/in place	✓	✓	✓	✓
Internal/external security procedures in place	✓	✓	✓	✓
Life cycle management plan	✓	✓	✓	✓

Tracking Lessons Learned

Table 10-2 includes an effective means of weekly tracking lessons learned, using an easy-to-update Excel spreadsheet. The preparer inserts the date at the top and the findings, with tracking numbers assigned. An arbitrary risk value is assigned, along with warnings, causes, recommended corrective actions; responsibilities and milestone dates.

Table 10-2. Tracking Lessons Learned on a Weekly Basis (Example Using an Excel spreadsheet)

Rev.	5		Operation:	Weekly Lessons Learned Report					
Date:	25-Oct		Sub-operation:	Construction - Pressure vessels					
Nr.	Event	Risk	Early Warning signs	Cause	Required Action(s)	Materiel/Non-Materiel	Responsibility	Completion Date	Status
C-1	HP welds		Failed welds; slag	Inadequate welder training/qualification	Prod. Dept review/ revise HP welder qualification	Materiel	Prod. Dept.	31-Jan	Qual. Prog. Revised
C-2	H.P. Fittings		Late arrival on-site	Vendor delays	Revise contract; replace vendor	Non-Materiel	Prod. Dept.	31-Dec	Bidding process begun
C-3	Safety Hazards		Workplace accidents	New/untrained employees	Conduct Safety Training; Re-certify safety equipment	Non-Materiel	Safety/HR	Ongoing	In progress
Prepared:		G. Smith		Reviewed:		J.P. Jones			
Date		25-Oct		Date		26-Oct			

Revision takes minimal f time, and can come from numerous sources.

The completed document may remain in electronic form throughout its life—on a computer screen and possibly on a projector. Trend graphs (e.g., of welders qualified) can be updated and attached for better understanding and tracking. There may be no need for hard copy distribution. The document not only forms the source for the monthly report, but for any other actions requiring a credible (positive or negative) justification.

Table 10-3 combines Figure 10-1 with Table 10-2 (again, readers can substitute their own inputs). We now have created a dynamic lesson learned "management tool" where perhaps only an "after-action report" had existed.

Table 10-3. Monthly Plotting of Lessons Learned with Program Management Requirements (Example Using an Excel Spreadsheet)

Program: Pressure Vessels				Monthly Lessons Learned Review (Not completed)				
Program Requirements vs. Lessons Learned	Risk Identification/Prioritization	Best Practices	Design Issues	Test planning/revision	Budget/Quality plans	Delivery shcedules	Manpower &Training Req'ments	Comments
Mission planning; concept development								
Design/development (including hardware/software)								
Modeling/Simulation								
Research & development								
Risk management plan								
Gap analysis								
Core team developed; responsibility/accountability assigned (including decision makers)								
Warfighter involvement								
Performance-oriented; metrics developed/consistent/actionable								
Test plans developed; tech yield identified								
Contract in place; executable								
Connectivity/feedback								Not established
Configuration/change management process defined/in place								
Internal/external security procedures in place								
Life cycle management plan								
Prepared:	Date:							
Reviewed:	Date:							

A lesson learned database spreadsheet model is a *multi-project* directory that you can edit to fit your program's needs. The model acts as the storehouse for all of your lessons learned across projects and throughout the program's life cycle. It can be used as reference as you start new projects, as your team looks for process improvements to make throughout the program, and to document successes and recurring issues in the projects as they happen.

To use this monthly report, just input the material from the weekly report, and add supporting information about the project, and any other relevant notes. Once you have input the lessons, you can filter and sort using the process categories and project type. You could even remove or add categories for simpler or more comprehensive sorting capabilities. Encourage your project team to exploit this model, add their own insights, and reference the lessons on future projects.

The Good—the Successes: What Went Right

"Lessons learned" often refers to failures and needed improvements to a team, a piece of equipment, or an operation. But it is just as important to capture the successes—but not just to celebrate. Successes often identify or reinforce best practices for the remainder of the program, future programs, projects, and processes. The (usually) expensive and hard-won knowledge should be shared. Everyone should learn and benefit.

Whether the success came from a short-term process change, a commitment to existing process, communication tweaks, or something else, it is worth documenting this to realize what "works" and can and should be carried on to the next project for you work and your team.

The Bad—the Failures: What Went Wrong

By "Bad" failures, I am thinking of materiel failures, which can come in the form of (to name a few):

- The inability of a product/system to achieve its desired results
- A higher-than-expected failure or breakdown rate or a diminished life cycle
- Problems with system/sub-system integration
- Unsafe product or system operation
- An unacceptable environmental footprint and/or a reduced product life cycle

Program managers and their bosses need to remember to fix the problem, and not to just fix the blame. The process is not punishment—it is management. A failure of any dimension must bring with it a realistic, actionable, solution—plus the assignment of a responsible individual or organization and a mechanism for assessing the effectiveness of the corrective action. Metrics and milestones are vital. Lives may depend on them.

The Ugly: What We Missed

"Ugly" means non-materiel failures that probably never should have occurred. It has been said: "Beauty is only skin-deep, but ugly goes right to the bone." So, what is an "ugly" failure? Here are a few examples:

- The program is over -budget
- The contract was awarded to the lowest bidder, period
- The contract was, in some form, not executable

- There is no funding fenced for training/simulation
- Milestones are unrealistic or meaningless
- There are no meaningful metrics.

Continual Improvement

Continual improvement is (or should be) the mainstay of any modern quality management system, especially in defense acquisition programs, as we commit to improving mission effectiveness by improving our product quality, employee communication, work environment, resources, and user satisfaction. All levels of the organizations participate; warfighter involvement is sought after and optimized.

Senior management provides the leadership, support, and resources to make continual improvement a priority. Middle management and process owners focus efforts and resources and review progress, and employees identify opportunities and recommend improvements. Figure 10-2 depicts the constancy of continual improvement.

Figure 10-2. Continual Improvement

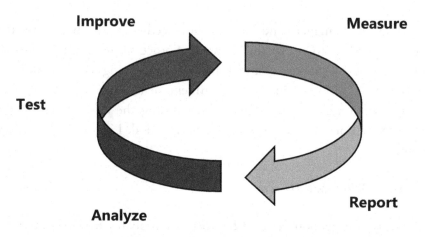

A continual improvement "mindset" drives the lessons-learned strategy for successful program management.

Ongoing data analysis, such as Six Sigma described in figure 10-3, can provide significant and actionable information on operational performance and improvement opportunities. Program managers review data, make decisions, and act on the findings provided by the data. Performance data, collected and analyzed with an Excel spreadsheet model, can provide real-time lessons learned, especially when the contract calls for manufacturing large quantities of precise products (e.g.; small arms ammunition).

Figure 10-3. Generic Six Sigma Presentation

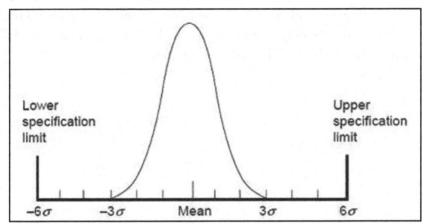

Summary

> *The only mistake in life is the lesson not learned.*
> *—Albert Einstein*

Capturing lessons learned is too important to be left until the end. By then it's too late for that program and probably for your next one as well.

Lessons learned should be captured, benefits and impacts analyzed with reference not only to the current program, but to future programs as well. You need to start at the top, with policies, procedures, and system steps—where both the positive and the negative are applied across a broad spectrum of government acquisition programs.

No process or product is so complex that it cannot be modeled and analyzed. In fact: the greater the complexity—the greater the need for analysis. If you need a database, make one, analyze it, and take action on what you find. Use all the tools at your disposal, including Excel and Six Sigma.

The best management practices that you create (or validate) in the lessons learned process confirm that you have identified the risks, and have done what you can to mitigate them.

The two most serious program manager mistakes that can make ineffective the lessons learned are to not include the participatory input of Warfighters and users and to wait until the end of the program to collect them.

Every program will have its "good," "bad," and "ugly." Identifying and minimizing the ugly will minimize the bad, and (in doing so) will maximize the good—and the earlier the better.

CHAPTER ELEVEN

Including Force Protection in the Program – The Challenges Continue

A "draw-down" of operating forces can mean an intensification of the force protection mission, requirement, or presence. Reduced numbers of operating forces remaining in forward operating bases will still require the same or even greater protection. They will be increasingly vulnerable to attack, due to reduced numbers, already-inadequate resupply and maintenance pipelines, and prolonged, open-ended, time remaining on station.

Regardless of the specific mission, operations not adequately planned or supported will take longer and increase force vulnerability, whereas well-planned and supported operations will leave forces exposed for shorter periods, and therefore *less* vulnerable.

When I went into the U.S. Navy in 1966, and for a long time before that, the operative catchphrase was: *"Damage Control is an all-hands responsibility."* The meaning was clear. Every member of the crew had both general and specific procedures to perform for the safety of the ship; spaces and equipment to maintain; instructions to follow; standards to reach or surpass, and examples to set. Maintenance was preventive and corrective. Non-performance of Damage Control aboard ship could mean mission degradation or loss of life. Possibly both.

> *A "draw-down" of operating forces can mean an intensification of the force protection mission, requirement, or presence.*

These days, the same could be said of *Force Protection*. It too is an all-hands' responsibility. In fact, it is both a primary and a support mission in all the Services, and will remain that way well into the future. The weapon of choice can be a sidearm or a computer; the vehicle can be a HUMVEE or a drawing table; the theater can be Afghanistan or El Paso.

The concept of Force Protection was initially created after the Beirut barrack bombings in Lebanon in 1983. With its Cold War focus toward potential adversaries employing large conventional military forces at the time (e.g., the Soviet Union), the U.S. military had become complacent and predictable with regard to asymmetric attacks by state and non-state actors employing terrorist and guerilla methodologies. As a result, during what were ostensibly peacekeeping operations by a U.S. Marine Corps landing force ashore in Lebanon in 1983, two civilian trucks breached the perimeter of the Marines' containment area and detonated their load of explosives as suicide vehicles adjacent to the Marine billeting areas.

Terrorist incidents over the years have shown a trend toward ever-increasing numbers of attacks and sophistication in methods. Terrorist methods include threats, bombing, kidnapping, hostage taking, hijacking, assassination, sabotage, arson, armed raids or attacks, and other measures to disrupt daily activities. Such actions occur rather routinely in some parts of the world, and almost anyone can become a potential victim. The attacks on the World Trade Center and Pentagon have shown that these attacks can occur within the United States as well.

DoD policy requires that all DoD military and civilian personnel and supporting defense contractors receive Antiterrorism/Force Protection (AT/FP) briefings before travel to any destination outside the United States. DoD contractors are to provide their personnel working on contracts outside the United States with AT/FP awareness information commensurate with that which DoD provides to its military and civilian personnel and their families.

This is the first of several articles based on Antiterrorism/Force Protection and security consulting work that I have been doing for a number of years, and describes how program managers need to understand the continuing requirement for robust force protection organization, equipment, training, and resupply.

There is often uncertainty among commanders tasked with force protection, as to the extent of the mission and their actual roles and responsibilities; and force protection roles and responsibilities may overlap with those of Antiterrorism and Self-defense. Accordingly, we need to begin with several basic definitions and relationships.

Antiterrorism (AT) describes *reactive* measures used to reduce the vulnerability of individuals and property to terrorist acts, to include limited response and containment by local military forces.

Force protection (FP) consists of *proactive* measures taken to mitigate hostile actions against Department of Defense and U.S. Coast Guard personnel (to include family members), resources, facilities, and critical information. Force protection was subsequently implemented throughout the Defense Department (and later adopted by the Coast Guard) to ensure that such a scenario never happened to U.S. forces again. Force protection itself is characterized by changing protective tactics to avoid becoming predictable.

Self-defense, in contrast, refers to the command or unit defending itself and the forces which make it up.

Figure 11-1 describes the interrelationship of antiterrorism, force protection, and self-defense.

Figure 11-1 Interrelationship of antiterrorism, force protection, and self-defense

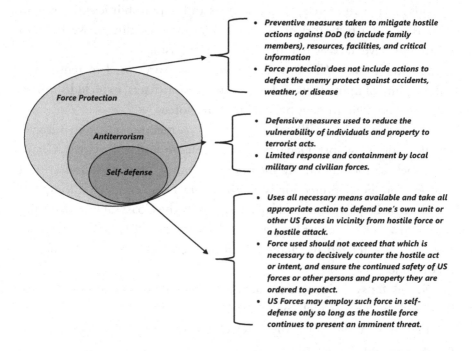

- Preventive measures taken to mitigate hostile actions against DoD (to include family members), resources, facilities, and critical information
- Force protection does not include actions to defeat the enemy protect against accidents, weather, or disease

- Defensive measures used to reduce the vulnerability of individuals and property to terrorist acts.
- Limited response and containment by local military and civilian forces.

- Uses all necessary means available and take all appropriate action to defend one's own unit or other US forces in vicinity from hostile force or a hostile attack.
- Force used should not exceed that which is necessary to decisively counter the hostile act or intent, and ensure the continued safety of US forces or other persons and property they are ordered to protect.
- US Forces may employ such force in self-defense only so long as the hostile force continues to present an imminent threat.

Figure 11-2 A deeper look at force protection and self-defense

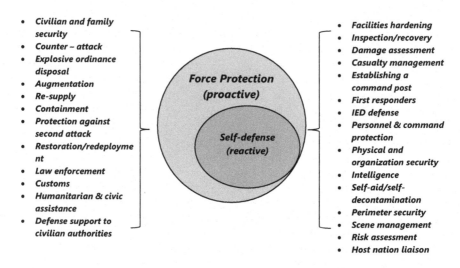

- Civilian and family security
- Counter – attack
- Explosive ordinance disposal
- Augmentation
- Re-supply
- Containment
- Protection against second attack
- Restoration/redeployment
- Law enforcement
- Customs
- Humanitarian & civic assistance
- Defense support to civilian authorities

- Facilities hardening
- Inspection/recovery
- Damage assessment
- Casualty management
- Establishing a command post
- First responders
- IED defense
- Personnel & command protection
- Physical and organization security
- Intelligence
- Self-aid/self-decontamination
- Perimeter security
- Scene management
- Risk assessment
- Host nation liaison

In figure 11-2, the bullets on the left are largely broad-based and general; those on the right are specific, as to a particular situation, place, or mission. The transition from general to specific, and (in doing so) from *proactive* to *reactive* is the work of mission planners and program managers working together.

Transition from proactive to reactive must be mission-specific. The force protection mission may be sub-set of an over-arching international mission, or it may exist by itself. Wherever it resides, there will always be a force protection mission for program managers to support – often after the original (i.e., more obvious) mission has been accomplished.

The next section describes how program managers and warfighters translate overarching strategies into actionable, albeit open-ended, force protection objectives. Also, the ongoing nature of force protection strongly suggests that program managers should cause review and revision the force protection mission routinely.

Developing/updating a force protection mission and concept of operations

As with figures 11-1 and 11-2, the terms in figure11-3 are well-known to program managers and warfighters. The mission (once accepted and authorized) necessitates the Concept of Operations, or CONOPS. Gaps are identified, comparing what must be done with what you have available to get it done, and courses of (corrective) action, or COAs come after that.

Figure 11-3 Developing the Force Protection CONOPS and TACSIT

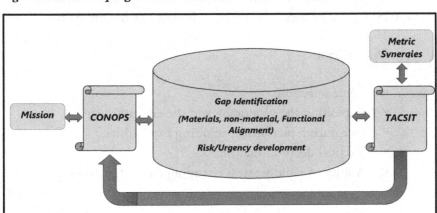

Threats, vulnerabilities, mission criticalities, (i.e., risks), and corresponding COAs cannot be assessed in the abstract. Findings and recommendations without real-world frames of reference would not be credible or supportable, despite the best efforts of subject matter experts.

The optimal method of developing the COAs without great expenditures of time and funds is the Tactical Situation or TACSIT.

TACSIT development

Again, there will be a continuing need for an AT/FP capability, if only to protect own forces, regardless of the location or projected scenario. Operating forces will be subject to attack, and increased time on station increases vulnerability. Regardless of the specific mission, operations not adequately planned or supported will take longer and increase force vulnerability, whereas well-planned and supported operations will leave forces vulnerable for shorter periods, and therefore *less* vulnerable. Forces will operate from forward operating bases, where only limited resupply and maintenance can take place. All the required force protection support will need to be tailored for the specific scenario – at the start and as long as the need continues.

TACSITs are scenarios based on real-world conditions used to shape and forecast future operations. TACSITs provide "value-adds" for program managers, often eliminating wasted time and resources by eliminating impractical approaches right at the gaming table. Modeling can be used in TACSITs when there is insufficient data or knowledge available.

TACSIT areas of focus should include (but not be limited to):

- Operational

    ✓ Force selection
    ✓ Exploiting the geography and the environment
    ✓ Integrating platforms/exploiting capabilities
    ✓ Tactical decision-making
    ✓ Ability to rapidly assess changing tactical situations

- Command

  ✓ Delegating authority (need for and ability to)
  ✓ Lines of communication
  ✓ Establishing information requirements for decision-making (i.e. The Commander's "Dashboard")
  ✓ Information processing
  ✓ Crisis response.

Several years ago, I helped to develop TACSIT scenarios for West Africa, Iraq, Cambodia, Straits of Hormuz, Indonesia, Philippines, South Korea, and Montenegro, based on likely deployments (and force protection requirements) of joint or composite commands.

Each location was an anticipated operating hot-spot region for the same contingency lead and support forces. "Materiel" solutions (new platforms and weapons) were barely in the design phase at that time. For that reason, the study group concentrated on "Non-materiel" and "Functional Alignment" solutions, and assessed their projected impact. We found that many problems for which new equipment was needed could, in fact, be mitigated to some extent by realigning forces and/or by rewriting operation orders and concepts of operations. It was in the rigorous development of non-materiel and functional alignment solutions that participants were better able to refine material requirements.

For example, movement of truck convoys in places like Iraq would be less vulnerable to attack if the current vehicles were replaced with some that offered increased armor protection and self-defense capabilities (materiel solution). However, routing those convoys around dangerous chokepoints and late at night (rather than in full daylight) also reduced vulnerability to attack (non-materiel solution). Required implementation cost and time: Negligible.

Threats were identified, risks assessed, and COAs are developed and examined. Risk *assessment* becomes risk *management* when participants evaluate the projected impact of the courses of action on the scenario.

Gaps, synergies, and metrics

Gaps are the differences between the level at which a capability is being performed currently and the level at which it must be performed to successfully accomplish the mission. Warfighters and program managers should be also alert for *overlaps* and *redundancies*. For example, when two subordinate commands establish separate logistics pipelines for the same parts, publish "almost identical" communication plans, or generate redundant reports.

Synergy is the combined or cooperative action of two or more stimuli for an enhanced effect, and that the whole becomes greater than the sum of its parts. Synergy can be quantified in subjective and objective metrics. *Innovation* is the introduction of something new or different, or the introduction of new things or methods. Program managers want innovation but may not recognize it or be able to quantify it.

Program managers must develop a synergy mindset that says "1 and 1 must equal 2.5 or it's not worth doing." The identification, quantification, and implementation of synergies are a vital product of the TACSIT. Representative synergies to look for include enhanced survivability; force multiplication; operational reach; and consolidation of like processes.

Metrics are the measurements used to monitor and to specifically, consistently, and uniformly, evaluate highly critical areas of your operations; in this case, gaps in force protection. Representative force protection gaps studies of my experience include:

- Speed of watercraft
- Response times and connectivity
- Weight of equipment (e.g.; body armor)
- Intercept ranges of sensors.

Courses of action

COAs are developed to correct identified gaps in the ability to carry out the force protection mission. COAs must address root causes of the gaps, and put corrective equipment, procedures, and/or practices in place to preclude or mitigate future occurrences. Additionally, COAs must bring with them the metrics and controls that ensure effective justification, implementation and operation.

Warfighters and program managers must generate and categorize COAs, with assigned metrics, milestones, and responsibilities; and then document them in a dynamic management tool, such as a plan of action and milestones. Once identified and screened thorough the TACSIT, the COAs are fed back into the CONOPS for further/continuing refinement, as shown in figure 3.

Table 11-1 provides a notional listing of the gaps, established COAs, measurable, replicable metrics from which to judge improvement, and the potential synergy achieved through COA implementation.

Table 11-1. Materiel, Non-Materiel and Functional Alignment Courses of Action (fictional)

Nr.	Capability Affected (fictional)	Identified by	Gap	COA	Metric	Synergies
M-01	NTA 6.2	Component cdrs.	Total operational Authority (TOA) is below needed level includes obsolescent equipment	Upgrade component command TOAs in numbers, suitability, and sustainment	Mission and on-station times (decrease)	Enhanced survivability, Force multiplication, operational reach, & like-process consolidation
NM-01	NTA 6.4	Component cdrs.	High attrition of qualified off/enl. with specific experience	Develop specializations and paths to promotion	Pers numbers and quals (increase)	Enhanced survivability, Force multiplication
FA-1	NTA 6.5,6.6	Component cdrs.	AT/FP training not centralized or specific	Develop standardized training pkgs (e.g., train the trainer)	Nr personnel trained/ quals (increase)	Enhanced survivability, Force multiplication

One example of each of the above three categories is shown for demonstration purposes. They are not the results of any particular study or exercise.

Summary

Force protection may be sub-set of an over-arching international mission, or it may exist by itself. Wherever it resides, there always will be a force protection mission – often after the original (i.e., more obvious) mission has been accomplished. The need for effective force protection personnel training, security, and supply chain management, will continue well into the future. The theater can be Afghanistan, El Paso, or anyplace in between.

The work of the Program Manager never ends. Regardless of the specific mission, operations not adequately planned or continually supported will take longer and increase force vulnerability; whereas well-planned and supported operations will leave forces vulnerable for shorter periods, and therefore *less* vulnerable and needing less protection.

TACSITs allow warfighters and program managers to take ideas, concepts, and procedures for a *test-drive*, with minimal expenditures of time and funding. They are "value-adds" that can eliminate impractical approaches right at the gaming table.

Warfighters and program managers must look for every opportunity to identify and implement synergies. Make 1 + 1 equal 2.5 or seriously consider dropping a program or program element.

Force protection courses of action must be *actionable*. Esoteric, impractical, or pie-in-the-sky musings on anybody's part have no place in a world in which real threats require real solutions, real soon.

CHAPTER TWELVE

The Ethical Imperative and the Courage to Cancel

> *The Ethical Imperative:*
> *Lives are at stake – either make the program*
> *work or make it go away!*

Looking back on an association of more than 40 years with the military (27 years spent on active duty) and a more than 50-year career in management, including time at the Pentagon; and then (most recently) reading the farewell writings of Under Secretary of Acquisition, Technology, and Logistics Frank Kendall, I am forced, unenthusiastically, to several conclusions.

- Some Department of Defense (DoD) acquisition problems come from Congress, and can thwart the best efforts of the most conscientious program managers.
- The same practices and procedures that characterize the successful management of acquisition programs can (and should) lead unapologetically to a decision to cancel those same programs.
- Technical and programmatic problems, sooner or later, have legal and ethical implications.
- "Sacred cows" make the best hamburger.

In 1982, as a young commander in the Pentagon and earlier having squandered my Navy career at sea, I tried to kill an overly bloated program for a mine countermeasures system. The program was devoid of meaningful milestones; the contract devoid of meaningful sanctions; and the vision devoid of meaningful reality. The delivered product would not have performed as required and sailors relying on it would have been endangered. The only indicators trending upward for the bloated program were the cost and the completion date. The Chief of Naval Operations wanted to kill it. Funds were tight, and we had many smaller, more cost-effective, "bread and butter" programs that could have used those funds. We wanted to put the funds to better use, for predictable and measurable benefits.

The prime contractor, who had established a plant in the home state of a member of the Senate Armed Services Committee, complained to the senator. Predictably, the senator directed that we put the funding back. Funding for the sensible but unglamorous programs was not his concern.

In 2006, as a military analyst for the Center for Naval Analyses (CNA), I worked on a program intended to develop sensors for detecting chemical and biological agents and to deploy those sensors in strategic ports of embarkation/debarkation (in the Middle East). The program was literally a "401k" for contractors, systems commands and "scientists" of all types. But it potentially endangered the lives of soldiers, sailors, and Marines. Field testing results were deceptive, and contractors tried lowering the bar to skew test results in their favor.

My decision briefing to my bosses at CNA ended with a slide bullet that read: "*We have an Ethical Imperative to withdraw our support from the program.*" I had never thought to use that term before. Management agreed, and we helped to drive a stake into the heart of a shameless, wasteful, and potentially dangerous program, in the meantime saving our own reputations.

The Ethical Imperative and the Best Guidance you could ever want

When Adm. James D. Watkins was tapped to return to Washington as Chief of Naval Operations, he brought back with him (then) Vice Admiral. Lee Baggett, Jr., to become Director of Naval Warfare. Watkins' guidance to Baggett to make the contentious and often antagonistic branch was: "*Either make it work or make it go away.*" Unsurprisingly, Baggett made it work. Watkins' guidance had a profound influence not only on an important branch of the Navy, but also on an unimportant young commander in the Pentagon's trenches. "Make it work or make it go away." What wiser guidance could ever be given, and what more welcomed guidance could ever be received?

Ethics in Program Management

For our purposes, consider "ethics" as a systematic reflection on rules and issues—the way people act and the rules that form the basis of their actions. Most of us endeavor to do what we believe is right. To drive safely for the benefit of pedestrians is *ethical*; to drive safely because *it is the law* is to fear a penalty and/or a punishment. Ethics come from *within* a person's moral sense and desire to preserve his or her self-respect. Legal requirements come from *outside the individual.* Organizational ethics (which I call Corporate Responsibility Management) institutionalizes reflection on those rules and issues, and then creates and controls all of its processes to ensure that the organization in questions perform to established ethical standards.

To operate "legally" is to operate in conformance with all established laws and regulations applicable to the mission of the organization. Laws and regulations are created by governments to protect their citizens.

Table 12-1 describes the work-a-day preoccupations of program managers and staffs. Since (theoretically at least) our laws reflect our ethical beliefs, you can adhere to both and violate both simultaneously.

An ethics-centered organization has an organizational "character" and strategy, taking very seriously not only its mission but also its responsibility to employees, customers, and the community.

Ethical violations may not result in punishment; legal violations carry punishment to the violators.

Table 12-1. Program Management Legal and Ethical Problem Areas

Problem Area	Legal	Ethical
Vision and Mission Development	✓	✓
Strategic Planning	✓	✓
Financial Management	✓	✓

Contract Management	✓	✓
Technology	✓	✓
Configuration Management	✓	✓
Research & Development	✓	✓
Risk Management	✓	✓
Supply Chain Management	✓	✓
Data Analyses	✓	✓
Training and qualification	✓	✓
Vendor Management	✓	✓

When program managers uncover legal problems, they create, *de facto*, an ethical imperative to take corrective action. Accordingly, it is virtually impossible to have only a legal problem or only an ethical problem.

Critical Thinking and Sound Judgment

In his last issue of *Defense AT&L*, Kendall also wrote about the need for critical thinking and sound professional judgment. To that, we now add *Ethical Imperative* and create. In figure 12-1, what you could call the three musketeers of program management. Like the slogan of Alexandre Dumas' courageous Three Musketeers of old: *One for all and all for one.*

Figure 12-1 The Triad of Program Management

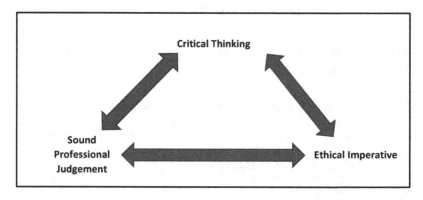

Critical thinking, according to Wikipedia, demands the ability to:

- Recognize problems, to find workable means for meeting those problems.
- Understand the importance of prioritization and order of precedence in problem solving.
- Gather and marshal pertinent (relevant) information.
- Recognize unstated assumptions and values.
- Comprehend and use language with accuracy, clarity and discernment
- Interpret data, to appraise evidence and evaluate arguments.
- Recognize the existence (or nonexistence) of logical relationships between propositions.
- Draw warranted conclusions and generalizations.
- Test one's conclusions and generalizations
- Reconstruct one's patterns of beliefs on the basis of wider experience.
- Render accurate judgments about specific things and qualities in everyday life.

In sum: "critical thinking is a persistent effort to examine any belief or supposed form of knowledge in the light of the evidence that supports or refutes it and the further conclusions to which it tends."

Sound professional judgement means our capacity to assess situations or circumstances wisely and to draw sound conclusions. This involves applying relevant training, knowledge and experience within the context provided by pertinent professional and technical standards, as applicable, in making informed decisions about appropriate courses of action.

Outside auditors (like me) are reminded continually of the requirement under international standards such as International Standards Organization 9000 to apply a structured skepticism throughout the audits.

Auditing, in this sense, is institutionalized and structured critical thinking, and refers to the appropriate application of professional skepticism.

Vision vs. Reality

Another part of Kendall's article concerned *vision vs. reality* and how important it is for a product or system to address the threats and employ the capabilities of the real world.

Figure 12-2 describes the transition of visions and missions into *actionable* systems and equipment through a series of sound program management processes. It also serves to remind the reader that conformity with sound management processes, de facto, creates an optimal environment for sound ethical decision making.

Figure 12-2. Vision vs. Reality

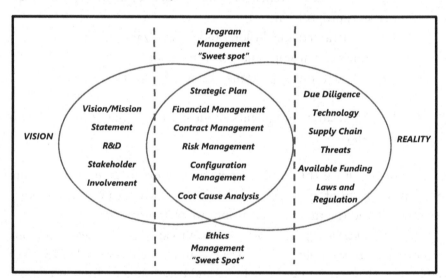

Requirements Analysis

Requirement analysis, for our purposes, means determining the needs or conditions to meet new or altered project requirements. Robust requirements analyses are essential to the success of a DoD acquisition program. The structure and outcome of the analyses must be documented, measurable and capable of being verified and validated. Most importantly, the analyses must create *actionable intelligence*, related to program needs and opportunities. Analyses must be clear, complete, consistent and unambiguous.

The findings of the (needs and) requirements analyses form the heart and soul of the contract, especially as reflected in the design, statement of work, and all the measurable goals and objectives. Milestones dates must be enforceable and enforced.

Due Diligence Due diligence can be defined as "investigation by or on behalf of an intended buyer, to check that the offeror has the desired assets, capabilities, technologies, brand rights, contracts, and other attributes required by the buyer and claimed as provided by the offeror. Put another way all the facts are available and have been verified. Areas for vendor due diligence audit and/or verification include (mentioning the big ones):

- Environmental and occupational safety and health compliance
- Corporate security (including cyber and information systems security)
- Manufacturing quality and competence
- Adherence to federal and state laws and regulations
- Budget monitoring and controls
- Supplier and supply chain management
- Code of ethics and standards of conduct
- The ability of investigate root causes of failures
- A robust set of internal controls
- Engineering and configuration management
- Capacity for growth or expansion.

A DoD decision to make a major purchase, acquisition or investment should reflect a comprehensive and structured due diligence process, custom-tailored for the specific undertaking. Regardless of the outcome, you will have given it your best shot.

Program Essentials

Table 12-2 lists fundamental acquisition program management requirements. Strength in all of them is essential; weakness in any of them should make a program fair game for critical review and possible cancellation. Moreover, the same DoD people expected to manage programs successfully should be encouraged to make their voices heard when cancellation is indicated.

The last row is the "Ethical Imperative." The program is satisfactory (SAT) if management recognizes and fosters it; unsatisfactory (UNSAT) if it does not exist.

Table 12-2. DoD Program Essentials

Program Essentials	SAT: Manage it	UNSAT: Cancel it
Program commitment at the top	✓	✓
Milestones	✓	✓
Metrics (e.g., Engagement Envelope)	✓	✓
Due diligence engrained in program	✓	✓
Vision and Mission vs Reality	✓	✓
Stakeholder Influence	✓	✓
Separate/related program interference	✓	✓
Contractor competence/motivation	✓	✓
Congressional Involvement	✓	✓
Risk Management Strategy	✓	✓
Requirements analyses	✓	✓
Benchmarking/gap analyses	✓	✓
Configuration management	✓	✓
Supply chain	✓	✓
Contract Structure (Cost Plus, FFP)	✓	✓
Contractor Code of Ethics and Standards of Conduct	✓	✓
ETHICAL IMPERATIVE – ALL PARTIES	✓	✓

Bullet-Proof, Bullet-Prone Bullet-worthy

Programs, as shown in figure 12-3, either at their inception or early in their implementation, predictably fall into one of three categories:

- Bullet-Proof because there is an unimpeachable vision, based on unimpeachable needs and requirements assessments, and containing realistic goals, and actionable objectives and milestones.

- Bullet-Prone because the vision is convincing, but does not reflect the needs and requirements assessments, and/or the metrics are lacking.
- Bullet-worthy because the even the most basic criteria described above are not measurably being met.

Figure 12-3. The" Bullet" Pyramid

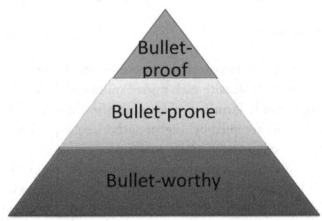

Figure 12-4 illustrates the ongoing necessity to monitor programs and to act forthrightly when action is necessary. Where is your program right now, and why?

Figure 12-4. Bullet-Proof, Bullet-Prone, or Bullet-Worthy—another View

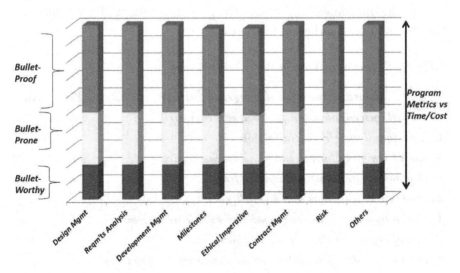

The breakdown of the bars is for illustration only, as are the notional areas being measured. The points to remember are:

- The soldier (sailor, airman, or Marine) is the primary stakeholder— not the member of Congress.
- Constant vigilance is the order of the day.

The Usual Suspects

Troubled programs don't get that way overnight. The signs are there and they become more visible with each missed milestone. Program managers and staffs know how to identify problems but often have difficulty making them known to (or accepted by) higher authorities, especially if the only way out appears to be canceling the program.

It is likely that many of the problems discussed thus far will be evident in a troubled program. It is just as likely that program managers can show in a documentable way when something started to go wrong and predictably determine the outcome.

This does not mean that the program manager's findings and recommendations, however quantifiable or actionable, will be accepted at the top of the totem pole.

Table 12-3 includes (cynically) historical causes that could have delayed, extended, weakened or otherwise trashed DoD programs, as seen by the outside world. Look at the possible causes and see if you can find the right one; and good luck proving it.

Table 12-3. Outsiders' View of What Went Wrong

Causes of potential program failure	Yes	No
Unethical/unscrupulous/unqualified contractor(s)	✓	
Congressional interference/direction	✓	
Systems Command bureaucracy and intransigence	✓	
Lack of milestone enforcement/discipline	✓	
Lack of top level support and due diligence	✓	
Vision, mission, operational capabilities unclear/'specious	✓	
Threat of protest and/or lawsuit by contractor	✓	
Inappropriate/unenforceable contract structure; mission creep	✓	

Needs analyses inappropriate/incomplete/non-existent	✓	
Budget cut/withheld	✓	
Tailored source selection	✓	
Lack of sanctions/penalties	✓	
Fraud, waste, and abuse – multi-level	✓	
INEFFECTIVE PROGRAM MANAGEMENT BY THE MILITARY		✓

The courage to cancel

Not inappropriately, the *decision* to cancel can only take place if there is the *courage* to cancel. The decision to cancel is the result of asking questions like these and getting the wrong answer:

- Is the program on track (with sound metrics, milestones realistic/met)?
- Is the contractor qualified and motivated, or did it just book the business?
- Have all the legal and ethical obligations been met?
- Does the program "vision" reflect reality?
- Is there excessive influence from stakeholders and higher authorities?
- Does the threat of protest or lawsuit permeate program operations?
- Is program risk excessive and/or unmitigated?

We have covered the justification for a decision to cancel. The courage to proceed after that has to come from the individual program managers and their chains of command. Take courage and good luck.

Summary

It was, is, and will always be, great sport to kill a program that does not measure up to requirements, especially when it is being sustained for the wrong reasons. Faithfully and diligently, program managers scrutinize their processes. In doing so, they predictably either *reinforce or expose* the underpinnings of their programs. When program managers uncover legal problems, they create, *de facto*, an ethical imperative to act. It is virtually impossible to have *only* a legal problem or *only* an ethical problem.

The same measuring rods that support a good program indict a bad one. The *ethical imperative,* that discomforting reminder to leaders and managers that when lives are at stake you either make the program work or make it go away, is both timeless and universal.

Simple? Of course! But why then is it applied so infrequently and ignored so frequently – at least at the top?

CHAPTER THIRTEEN

Second-Party Audit of Government Contracts

Ten areas for no-nonsense contractor auditing by DoD program managers

An *audit* is a systematic, independent, and documented process for obtaining objective evidence and evaluating it to determine the extent to which program criteria (policies, procedures, or requirements) have been fulfilled.

There are three types of audits.

- A **first-party audit** is performed within an organization to measure its strengths, weaknesses, and conformance with established standards. This is also called an *internal* audit. Internal audits satisfy internal requirements and audit results remain in-house.

- A **second-party audit** is an external audit performed on a supplier by a customer or by a contracted organization on behalf of a customer. In second-party audits (for our purposes) DoD program managers measure and evaluate the DoD contractor's ability to conform to contract requirements and specifications.

- A **third-party audit** is performed by an audit organization independent of both the contractor and DoD and is free of all conflicts of interest. Third-party audits (e.g., by an International Standards Organization ((ISO)) Registrar) may result in certification, registration, or award certificate issued by the third party.

This chapter discusses second-party audits; specifically, wherein DoD program managers *audit* their contractors' ability to execute the contract. I strongly recommend that program managers incorporate second-party audits into DoD contacts, regardless of contract size, scope, or final deliverable.

> ### *Audits must have objectives, scope, and criteria.*
> ### *Anything less is a waste of time.*

Like the organizations or contracts that they address, the audits themselves must have objectives, scope, and criteria. Anything less is a waste of time. Figure 13-1 summarily describes a comprehensive program of second-party audits. Note especially the inclusion of "Operators & Warfighters". This inclusion alone distinguishes effective second-party auditing from routine program management. Participation by experienced, credible, operators/end-users help to ensure that programs do not stray from the goals of the contract or the purpose of the end products.

Figure 13-1 Second-party audit of DoD contracts by DoD program management

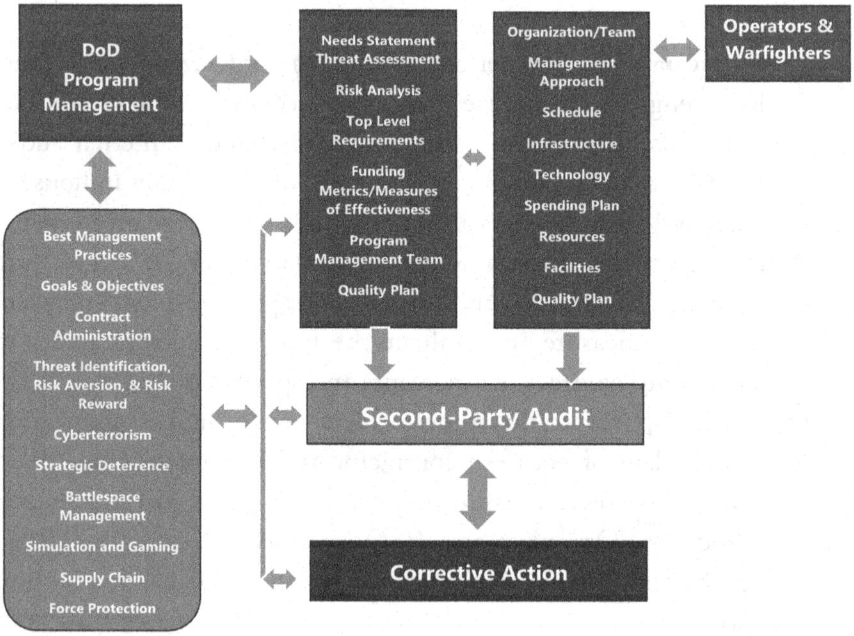

Active operator involvement throughout the DoD program can correct problems in the early stages or preclude them altogether. It's much better to find a problem with a product or program stateside than in-theater. That said, engineers don't always welcome operator input.

Anything is fair game in a second-party audit; just don't waste time in the wrong places or fail to take action on the audit findings.

Ten Areas for Auditing

1. Best management practices

The ISO family of international management standards (each of which contains internal and external auditing guidance) includes not only specific "conformance to standard" requirements for certification purposes, but also discrete, traditional, management practices instituted in the better organizations. They include strategic planning, statistical process control, environmental management and compliance, occupational safety and health, risk management, root cause identification, cost-benefit analysis, life cycle analysis, training, and performance/effectiveness measurement and improvement.

Today's political and economic conditions require development and implementation of additional, more contemporary considerations to further focus product development and to keep it focused - as shown in figure 13-2. These additional considerations require no definition or explanation.

Figure 13-2 Additional best management practice considerations

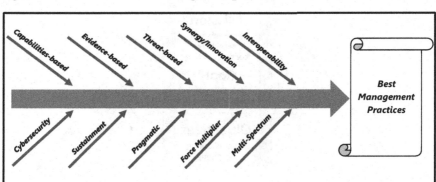

DoD contracts should reflect both the traditional and the contemporary best management practices and considerations, in provable, measurable, arrangement.

> *Achievement of <u>DoD</u> goals and objectives is not possible without achievement of <u>contractor</u> goals and objectives, which should essentially be the same.*

2. Program and contractor goals and objectives

Goals and objectives allow private sector organizations to do (among many other things) stay in business, grow and develop in a sustainable manner, and create or revise processes that create products, services, or (in some other way) value. They also reduce costs, manage competition, manage risk, and maintain credibility with stakeholders.

In an earlier edition of this magazine, I wrote about auditing (DoD) goals and objectives. The type of audit I described was a *first-party* audit. Figure 13-3 reviews the makeup and relationship of program goals and objectives. Each is both a function of and dependent upon the others. Review and reevaluation of goals and objectives are continuous and a change or revision in one requires change or revision is the others.

Figure 13-3. Program and contractor goals and objectives

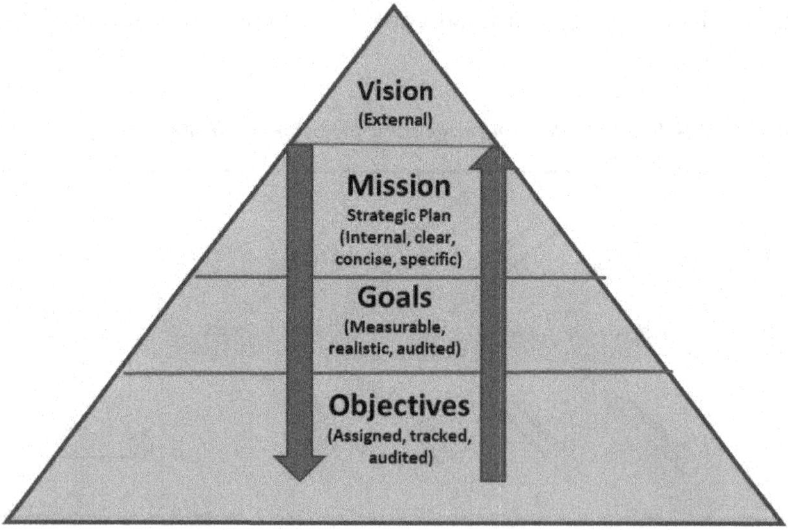

For purpose of the specific contract, the contractor goals and objectives should essentially be the same as those of DoD; and easily measurable in a second-party audit. Achievement of DoD goals and objectives is not possible without nearly simultaneous achievement of contractor goals and objectives.

The best way to ensure that the objectives will continue to receive attention and corrective action when required is to go to the last step in the planning process, and create the Plan of Action and Milestones, or POA&M. An effective POA&M contains key completion dates, responsible individuals/departments, follow-up strategies, and the objective metrics. POA&Ms (or whatever they are called) should be assessed in a second-party audit.

3. Contract administration

Contract administration lends itself exceptionally well to internal and external audit. Checklists track contracts through all the necessary review processes. Audit findings, shortfalls, and required corrective actions, are juxtaposed next to their associated quantifiable and auditable contract requirements (e.g., completion/delivery dates, performance metrics, reliability tests).

The future of the Country in general, and the DoD in particular, requires a rock-solid industrial base; and DoD can optimize that rock-solid industrial base only as long as the contracts that bind DoD to that base are well administered, as described in figure 13-4. Meaningful information exchange is the life's blood of the contract, and must flow constantly in both directions.

Figure 13-4 The industrial base of DoD contracting

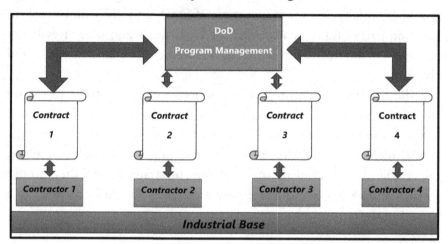

Recurring progress reports, critical in contract administration, often don't identify problems in the early stages, and are seldom the *management tools* that they were intended to be. Problems are masked, threats and risks not tracked, data lost, and trends not spotlighted.

In short, recurring reports required by contracts don't always talk about the *bad stuff*. And there is always bad stuff. Second-party audits not only audit the program, but validate the reports. Moreover, audit reports may actually replace more traditional reporting formats.

4. Risk aversion and risk - reward

We are used to the terms *risk analysis, risk assessment,* and *risk management.* Often used interchangeably, they can describe a variety of different approaches and/or metrics. *Risk aversion* and *risk – reward* are two recent additions to contract verbiage, but with essentially the same meaning.

There is no one single approach to handling risk, nor should there be. The challenge to management is to frame the output of its risk analyses in a manner that makes sense to the decision makers and that clearly and concisely identifies the threat, represents the present and predicts the future. Approaches and strategies can be as simple or complex as the processes they were made to assess. However, simpler is almost always better, and using a spreadsheet model that automatically computes and displays the assessments is better still, as shown in figure 13-5.

Figure 13-5 Risk computation and adjustment (an example)

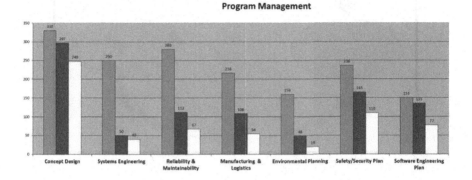

A spreadsheet model, like that depicted in figure 13-5, can be updated and distributed immediately and can replace the slow-moving recurrent report.

The depth and scope of a risk validation is a function of the organization's risk assessment strategy and approach. Even if no other good reason existed, the requirement to continually re-assess an organization's *risk* is reason enough to continually validate/re-validate all the metrics and measures of effectiveness used by the organization, as depicted in figure 13-6.

Figure 13-6 Risk validation

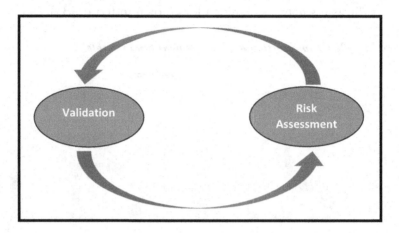

5. Cyber terrorism and software development

Organizations, whether military and civilian, that cannot conduct their operations in a self-imposed and self-monitored secure environment may cease to exist just as certainly as organizations that cannot maintain operational effectiveness, profitability, or product or service superiority – only faster. They must *harden* their operations to protect them from either incidental or deliberate attack. Second-party *security* audits (up to and including penetration testing as an example) ensure that hardening processes are in place at all facilities involved in the DoD contract.

ISO 27000 and ISO 28000, *Information Systems Security Management* and *Supply Chain Security Management* respectively, provide excellent collections of ready-to-use, measurable, security guidance (with checklists) for everything from computer software to shipping containers. These International Standards can make you an effective auditor with your first audit.

6. Strategic deterrence

Strategic deterrence is intended to dissuade an adversary from taking an action not yet started by means of the threat of reprisal; or to prevent them from doing something that another state desires.

The use of strategic deterrence as a means to discourage international crises and war has been a central focus of U.S. international security for at least 200 years. Research has predominantly focused on the theory of rational deterrence to analyze the conditions under which conventional deterrence is likely to succeed or fail. Alternative theories however have challenged the rational deterrence theory and have focused on organizational theory and cognitive psychology.

DoD programs must contain a deterrent capability that supports viable offensive and defensive U.S. strategy.

7. Battlespace management – the warfighter as auditor

Again, meaningful auditing of DoD programs must include a warfighter's assessment of how the programs address "battlespace management", or *who does what - and where.*

Warfighter commanders and planners develop standard operating procedures (SOPs), concepts of operation (CONOPS), and checklists, that reduce the battlespace management to workable and replicable practices and procedures, chains of command, and communications networks. It follows that they add significant value, realism, and (perhaps) a sense of urgency to product development and roll-out.

Warfighter logisticians audit supply chains for normal and surge operations in accordance with the threat scenarios, timelines, weather, and the environment. They also take a critical look at technological "yield." That is: do the resources, however complex, optimally and successfully accomplish the missions, or is a greater capability required.

8. Simulation and gaming

Earlier issues of this magazine covered replacing case studies with simulations, wherein modeling and testing scenarios replace static representations of historical conditions, now overtaken by events.

The gaming and simulation that the wargame or tabletop provides can be an effective initial step to deliberate program goals and objectives as well as address the full range of issues related to the product(s) to be developed – in operational or even crisis scenarios. These exercises provide a relevant, credible, and consequential forum to examine roles and responsibilities, unearth synergies and interdependencies, develop needs and risk assessments, and to evaluate contingency plans.

Highly cost-effective wargames or tabletop exercises bring in all the key players – strategists, engineers, logisticians, and operators.

9. Continual Improvement

"Continual Improvement", the basis and underpinning of the ISO International Standards, must be thought of as an ongoing process and not an "end state". It requires program managers and contractors to develop a *mindset* that says that we can always make something better.

Continual improvement of organizational security for example requires top management to review the organization's security management system at planned intervals, in order to ensure its continuing suitability, adequacy, and effectiveness. Second-party audits and reviews should include assessing opportunities for improvement and the attendant need for changes to the program management system, including policies, objectives, threats, and risks.

10. Force protection

For purposes of this article, force protection means preventive measures taken to mitigate or preclude hostile actions against Department of Defense and U.S. Coast Guard personnel, resources, facilities, and critical information. The concept of Force Protection was initially created after the Beirut barrack bombings in Lebanon in 1983. *It* represents the programs, processes, and procedures, that are designed to *protect* military members, civilian employees, family members, facilities, and equipment.

These days, virtually any DoD program should acknowledge and address the attendant need for a viable force protection strategy in all developmental and operational stages of a product's life cycle.

Audit Structure

Table 13-1 summarizes the basic audit structure.

Table 13-1 Second party audit structure

Component	Explanation	Example
Scope	Contract deliverable being audited	Training simulator, software, & manual
Reference	Applicable contract/subcontract technical standard	Section XX. 1
Location(s)/ Department(s)	Where the work to be audited is focused	Jacksonville Assembly facility
Audit team	DoD designed auditors	OPNAV XX/NAVSEA XX
Kick-off Brief	Introductions/discussions/ commencement	0900 12 July in CEO's office
Audit Conduct (Phase i)	Team and counterparts review applicable process(es) against established references; identify deficiencies; debriefs at end of each day	Assembly and/or calibration process
Audit Conduct (Phase ii)	Auditors summarize results; develop and categorize findings/observations; develop recommendations; prepare audit report	Confirm findings and check against refs; repeat observations where necessary
Preliminary debrief	Team Leader(s) brief DoD and contractor top management	Private debriefing of DoD and CEO
Formal debrief	Scheduled; Audit team debriefs all affected personnel; discusses final report	1600 15 July in CEO's office
Publish Final Report	Finding/observations; corrective action and completion dates; date of re-audit if necessary	POA&M

** POAM: Plan of action and Milestones*

ISO audits simply but effectively classify findings as "major" or minor". Major findings either involve safety or some other compelling condition, and dictate that they be corrected as soon as possible. Minors contribute to defective end-products or services, but can be correct in the normal course of events. "Observations" are not actual findings but spotlight potential problem areas. Observations can also be the origination point for continual improvement.

It is essential that each finding have a corrective action, an assignment of responsible personnel/departments, a completion date, and a follow-up scheme to ensure that the "corrective action" does, in fact correct the problem.

Summary

You can expect the prospect of an additional form of oversight to meet with resistance from contractors. Similarly, you can expect your own planners and engineers to resist a "fleet input" from operators and warfighters. Resistance will give in to persistence, and the kind of measurable product improvement that comes from effective second-party auditing will make the case for the program manager. It's much better to find a problem with a product or program stateside than in-theater.

As an auditor and consultant for five ISO management systems for over 25 years (not to mention the 27 years of Naval service before that), I have seen the advances and successes that come from structured internal and external auditing strategies and programs. Regrettably, I've seen just as many instances where failure to take corrective action compounded problems and caused major delays or failures – even actual and potential losses of life.

CHAPTER FOURTEEN

Toward a Performance (and Quality)-Based Adaptive Acquisition Framework – AAF meets ISO

As stated in Department of Defense (DoD) Instruction 5000.02 of Jan. 23, 2020: "the Adaptive Acquisition Framework (AAF) supports the DoD with the objective of delivering effective, suitable, survivable, sustainable, and affordable solutions to the end user in a timely manner. To achieve those objectives, Milestone Decision Authorities (MDAs), other Decision Authorities (DAs), and Program Managers (PMs) have broad authority to plan and manage their programs consistent with sound business practice. The AAF acquisition pathways provide opportunities for MDAs/DAs and PMs to develop acquisition strategies and employ acquisition processes that match the characteristics of the capability being acquired."

There's more!

"Performance Based Acquisition (PBA) is a method of preparing service contracts that emphasizes *the service outcomes the Government would like the contractor to provide.* The use of PBA has been encouraged by the Office of Management and Budget to drive down the costs of contracts while improving contractor performance."

What that means for PMs is that DoD tells contractors *what* capability it wants, and then leaves it to them to determine *how* to satisfy that capability.

Does that make life easier for PMs, or help to ensure a product built most efficiently —on time and within budget? Not by itself. In fact, it

135

exchanges one set of concerns for another set, and leaves policing the contracts and creating a quality product as challenging as ever.

> *Word searches for terms such as: quality, audit, verification, and validation will get you: "No matches were found" for both directives.*

The two primary directives of the AAP are (1) DoD Directive (DoDD) 5000.01 The Defense Acquisition System (DAS); and (2) DoDI 5000.02: Operation of the Adaptive Acquisition Framework.

DoDD 5000.01 prescribes that the DoD will:

... employ the following operating policies:

1. *Simplify acquisition policy*
2. *Tailored acquisition approaches*
3. *Empower PMs*
4. *Conduct data-driven analysis*
5. *Actively manage risk*
6. *Emphasize sustainment.*

We will go into each of these six directed operating policies in the sections that follow. Two realities will form the basic theme of this writing:

1. The directives provide little guidance regarding *how* to realize these policies, leaving it to PMs.
2. Word searches for the following fundamental management terms: quality, audit, verification, validation, feedback, follow-up, and accountability, will get you: *"No matches were found"* for both directives.

A word search of other fundamental program management catchwords, such as *measurement, objectives, risk,* and *performance,* will lead the reader to an appropriate number of matches in all the appropriate places. So, there is hope. Our job is to support the catchwords with a solid underpinning of sound management practices used successfully over many years by forward-thinking companies in the private sector. PMs can do this by planning a quality management system and making it part of the AAF in general and each acquisition project in particular.

The International Organization for Standardization (ISO) is a worldwide federation of national standards bodies. The work of preparing International Standards, such as those discussed herein is carried out by technical committees, in response to demand from industry. Independent certification bodies "certify" organizations to applicable ISO Standards, and, in doing so, attest to the effectiveness of the organization as a responsible provider of quality goods and services.

Government contractors (e.g., shipyards, weapons manufacturers) who certify to applicable ISO Standards are more likely to successfully deliver a "quality" product—on time and within budget. ISO-Certified contractors often receive (appropriately) the inside track in the awards process. Many DoD contracts specifically require contractor applicants to be certified to one of the Standards prior to the proposal submission date. This can be a "value-add" for both DoD and the contractors. However, it also can lead to what we auditors call "Just-in-time Certification," which is often perfunctory. The ink on the certificate is barely dry, and there is no track record of documented ISO-acceptable performance. An organization certified to any of the ISO Standards, in my opinion, requires about one year of implementation actual practice, and self-audit before the Standard reaches its maximum contribution.

I have been a practicing ISO auditor and consultant since 1996, and remain a staunch advocate. PMs/staffs can download the ISO Standards (available online) to develop and implement viable program management in accordance with the AAF. The Standards will help PMs with the "How" component of program management; they do not add anything to the "What" component. They do not require any additional work from PMs. In fact, streamlining already existing areas such as "risk management," "internal auditing," "reports management," and "goals and objectives," routinely reduce wasteful or redundant effort for certified organizations.

Explaining any (or all) of the ISO Standards is too great an undertaking for this article. Tables 1 and 2 will give you the idea. Suffice it to say that the Standards mentioned here have clauses that provide excellent guidance for the development and operation of quality management systems. If you are not familiar with the ISO family of International Standards, maybe you need to learn about them, and if your vendors are not ISO-certified, maybe they should be.

Where AAF Meets ISO

Table 14-1 takes the six "operating policies" of the AAF (source: DoDD 5000.01) and recommends appropriate ISO support processes. Here is where AAF meets ISO.

Table 14-1. AAF Operating Policies Meet ISO Standards

Nr	AAF Operating Policies (Ref: DoDI 5000.02)	ISO 9000 Quality Management System Clauses.*	Applicable ISO Standard
1.	Simplify Acquisition Policy	Quality policies, goals, & objectives; Risk-based thinking; environmental aspects; Implementation & operation; Continual Improvement; Product/process development	1,2,3,4
2.	Tailor Acquisition Approaches	Quality, policies, goals, & objectives; Operational planning & control; Design & development controls	1,2,3,4
3.	Empower Program Managers	Quality policies, goals, & objectives; Management review; Internal audit; checklist development; Communication Feedback, follow-up, & accountability;	1,2,3,4
4.	Conduct Data-driven Analysis	Quality policies, goals, & objectives; Information systems and Supply chain security management targets, data analysis & evaluation; Performance evaluation; Control of changes; Measurement and traceability	1,2,3,4
5.	Actively Manage Risk	Risk-based thinking; Quality policies, goals, & objectives; Threats, criticalities, & vulnerabilities; Establish acceptable/unacceptable risk parameters; Control of nonconforming product	1,2,3,4
6.	Emphasize Sustainment	Quality policies, goals, & objectives; Implementation & operation; Continual Improvement; Nonconformity & corrective action; Preservation	1,2,3,4

> **ISO Standards**
> 1. ISO 9000: Quality Management Systems
> 2. ISO 14000: Environmental Management Systems
> 3. ISO 27000: Information Security Management Systems
> 4. ISO 28000: Supply Chain Security Management Systems

* Note: The other three Standards have similar clauses

> *"Put the emphasis on the results to be*
> *achieved—the deeds to be done."*
> *—Quality management consultant and engineer Joseph M. Juran*

Here is a deeper look into the AAF operating policies and ISO requirements that address them.

1. Simplify acquisition policy

It's reassuring to remember that even the most complicated strategic acquisition policy for the most complicated government program can be managed using quality evangelist Joseph M. Juran's basic formula for getting results:

a. Establish specific goals to be reached.
b. Establish plans for reaching the goals.
c. Assign clear responsibility for meeting the goals.
d. Base the rewards on the results achieved.

Acquisition policies need only to satisfy these four criteria. Goals must be "aimed-at" targets, toward which all the effort is expended. This is how you "simplify" the acquisition policy. The ISO Standards provide excellent structure to acquisition policy formulation, by adding the ability to *measure* success through programs such as internal (self) audit, management review, risk management, data collection and analysis, corrective action, and feedback.

2. Tailor Acquisition Approaches

PMs are told to consider acquisition approaches that leverage international acquisition and supportability planning to improve economies of scale, strengthen the defense industrial base, and enhance coalition partner capabilities to prepare for joint operations.

The actual type of contract is often a done deal long in advance of approach development. Similarly, regulatory requirements are not open for discussion. Accordingly, our focus is on what the approach must include, regardless of the type of the contract. Space limitations preclude lengthy discussion here, but PMs need to focus on time and security. Acquisition approaches are a function of the mission and its urgency; and time and security will always be vital to the "tailoring" (i.e., streamlining) process(es). The more urgent the Warfighter's mission—the more tailored the approach.

3. Empower PMs

PMs are expected to plan their acquisition programs in a thoughtful, innovative, and disciplined manner. Library shelves are filled with recommended approaches— some appropriate and some not. Not mentioned is the amount of empowerment given and the form that it takes, nor the manner in which program progress is measured.

The ISO Standards, when employed by PMs, not only empower, but provide defensible measurements of success and the justifications for actionable correction. Clause 9.3: Management Review, and Clause 5.1: Leadership and Commitment of the latest ISO 9000 Standard provide the foundation for an effective and successful program for "empowered" management. Following the steps of the clauses creates uncomplicated programs, leading to quality products, by way of solid processes and acceptable risks.

I commanded a U.S. Naval Station in the late 1980s. "Environment" and "Ecology" were the catchwords, and the "Responsible Line Commander" was in the cross-hairs. We were not even told *what* to do, let alone *how* to do it. We were only promised that an environmental incident (e.g., harbor pollution) meant loss of job and career and maybe even a civil lawsuit. I developed a set of checklists and wrote an instruction for the subordinate and tenant commands, and then I set up an audit/inspection process. My boss and I kept our jobs, but what I would have given for an environmental management system like ISO 14000 back then. The first version of ISO 14000: Environmental Management Systems appeared in 1996.

4. Conduct Data-Driven Analysis

DoDI 5000.02 directs that product support/PMs: "make use of data-driven decision-making tools with appropriate predictive analysis capabilities to improve systems availability and reduce costs." Again, it leaves the managers on their own with regard to *how* to collect the data, *from what sources*, and *what to do* with the data once collected; and little incentive other than the threats that come with no usable data collected.

ISO 9001:2015 (operative version) Clause 9.1.3: "Analysis and Evaluation" guides PMs and staffs through the data collection and analyses process, giving collected data purpose and utility. Equally important, it guides PMs away from collection and/or reliance on meaningless, misleading, or otherwise irrelevant data.

5. Actively Manage Risk

DoD tasks PMs to: "Establish a risk management program to ensure program cost, schedule, and performance objectives are achieved, and to communicate the process for managing program uncertainty. In consultation with the user representative, the PM will determine which environment, safety, and occupational health risks must be eliminated or mitigated, and which risks can be accepted."

ISO 9001:2015 Clauses 4.4.1 (f) and 6.1 describe *"risks and opportunities."* It is in the coupling of these two terms that PMs can assure themselves that their quality management system can achieve its desired results, enhance its desired effects, prevent/reduce undesired effects, and achieve continual improvement.

ISO 28001:2007 describes *"risk-based thinking"* when dealing with security risks in the supply chain.

6. Emphasize Sustainment

DoDD 5000.01 requires DoD Components to acquire systems, subsystems, equipment, supplies, product support, *sustainment*, and services in accordance with the statutory requirements for competition. Defining "sustainment" itself and in relation to other terms (e.g., life cycle) remains a challenge for the PM. However, an ISO 9000-based Quality Management System (in the aggregate) *is* a Sustainment Plan. Table 14-2 includes some of the ISO 9000 clauses that would help to create both a comprehensive Quality Management System (QMS) and a viable Sustainment Plan.

Table 14-2. Using ISO 9000 to Create a Sustainment Plan

ISO 9000 Clause	Clause Title	QMS	Sustainment Plan
4.3	Scope of the quality management system	✓	✓
4.4	Quality management system and its processes	✓	✓
5.1	Leadership and Commitment	✓	✓
5.2.1	Establishing a quality policy	✓	✓
6.1.2 (a)	Actions to address risks and opportunities	✓	✓

6.2	*Quality objectives and planning to achieve them*	✓	✓
7.1.5.2	*Measurement and traceability*	✓	✓
8.1	*Operational planning and control*	✓	✓
8.3	*Design and development of products and services*	✓	✓
8.7	*Control of nonconforming outputs*	✓	✓
9.1	*Monitoring, measurement, analysis, and evaluation*	✓	✓
9.2	*Internal audit*	✓	✓
9.3	*Management review*	✓	✓
10.3	*Continual improvement*	✓	✓

> ## *ISO: Triumph of Titanium Over Boilerplate.*

Table 14-3 compares four of the ISO family of Quality Management Systems (QMS) with the "Tenets" of the Defense Acquisition System, as described in DoDI 5000.02.

Table 14-3. Applying Some ISO/QMS Processes to AAF Tenets

ISO /QMS Process	Materiel solutions analysis	Technology Maturation & Risk reduction	Engineering & Manufacturing development	Production & Deployment
Internal Audit/Checklist development	1,2,3,4	1,2,3,4	1,2,3,4	1,2,3,4
Risk Management	1,2,3,4	1,2,3,4	1,2,3,4	1,2,3,4
Management Review	1,2,3,4	1,2,3,4	1,2,3,4	1,2,3,4
Process Mapping	1,2,3,4	1,2,3,4	1,2,3,4	1,2,3,4
Process Validation & Verification	1,2,3,4	1,2,3,4	1,2,3,4	1,2,3,4
Feedback, follow-up, & accountability	1,2,3,4	1,2,3,4	1,2,3,4	1,2,3,4
Certification	1,2,3,4	1,2,3,4	1,2,3,4	1,2,3,4

Materiel Development Decision → Operations and Sustainment

1. ISO 9000: Quality Management Systems
2. ISO 14000: Environmental Management Systems
3. ISO 27000: Information Security Management Systems
4. ISO 28000: Supply Chain Security Management Systems

The four International Standards support and complement each other; and provide useful guidance for virtually any DoD program or contract.

SUMMARY (Part I)

Check out these two quotes:

1. *DoDD 5000.01, Sept. 9, 2020: "Joint concepts, standardization, and integrated architectures will be used to the maximum extent possible to characterize the exchange of data, information, materiel, and services to and from systems, units, and platforms to assure all systems effectively and securely interoperate with other U.S. forces and coalition partner systems".*
2. *DoDI 5000.02, Jan. 23, 2020: "Under the supervision of PMs, product support managers develop, plan, and implement a comprehensive product support strategy for all integrated product support elements and their material readiness. Product support managers will make use of data-driven decision-making tools with appropriate predictive analysis capabilities to improve systems availability and reduce costs."*

The DoD directives provide guidance about "what to do," but little direction regarding "*how* to do it" (or even how do you know when you *have* done it), leaving it to program managers; and word search of the following terms: "quality", "audit", "verification", and "validation" will get you: *"No matches were found"* for both directives.

The most complicated government program can be managed successfully using Juran's basic formula for getting results:

a. aEstablish specific goals to be reached.
b. bEstablish plans for reaching the goals.
c. cAssign clear responsibility for meeting the goals.
d. dBase the rewards on the results achieved.

The ISO Quality Management Standards and clauses designated in the tables provide excellent direction for the development and operation of effective quality management systems in full compliance of AAF requirements, and full support of DoD programs.

Many DoD contracts specifically require contractor applicants to be certified to one of the Standards prior to the proposal submission deadline.

"Just-in-time certification" is often perfunctory, with no track record of documented ISO-acceptable performance.

An organization certified to any of the ISO Standards, in my opinion, requires about one year of implementation, execution, and self-audit before it reaches its maximum contribution.

The ISO Standards are available online. You can order/download them in the time it took to read this. If you are not familiar with the ISO family of International Standards, maybe you need to learn about them; and if your vendors are not ISO-certified, maybe they should be.

Part II: Ten ways to get off to the right start

The two primary directives of the Adaptive Acquisition Framework (AAF) are (1) DoDD 5000.01 The Defense Acquisition System (DAS); and (2) DoDI 5000.02: Operation of the Adaptive Acquisition Framework. Both are comprehensive, prescriptive, vague, and ponderous.

The DoD directives provide well-meaning but weighty guidance about "what to do," but little useful assistance regarding "*how* to do it" (or even how do you know when you *have* done it), leaving it to program managers; and word search of the following terms: "quality", "audit", "verification", and "validation" will get you: *"No matches were found"* for both directives.

This is a Part II to my previous article concerning the pertinency and utility of the ISO International Standards alongside the requirements of the AAF. In this article and the last, I hope to convince readers in general and program managers in particular to use The International Standards Organization (ISO) management standards. These are tried, tested, and ready-to-go standards, that provide structure and direction for both the creation and execution of DoD acquisition contracts – fulfilling (and clarifying) AAF requirements.

In the past, I have written about and stressed the need for the following competencies in management of DoD programs:

- Risk management and gap analysis
- Operator and/or warfighter participation
- Meaningful feedback, follow-up, and accountability

- Modeling and simulation, including tabletop exercises and/or wargames
- Contingency and continuity planning
- Working through and after a pandemic
- Second party auditing.

These competencies (and *mindsets*) are endemic to the ISO programs and where AAF can meet ISO.

> *A credible, no-nonsense, working document and indispensable management tool would replace an often contrived and superficial work of "semi-fiction."*

When ISO 9001:1994 (the first iteration, already positively received in Europe and Asia) was introduced inside the Beltway, the strategy was that ISO 9000-Certified contractors could simply submit copies of their (already existing) quality manuals in response to requests for proposal (RFP) – foregoing forever the need for creating those great tomes of questionable veracity known as *proposals*. Proposals ask the question: "How would you solve *my* problem if you get the contract?" Quality manuals answer the question: "What service are you *already providing for all your clients?*"

Quality manuals (and/or operating procedures (OPs)) developed in accordance with ISO 9000 (for example) must meet, initially and periodically, the certification requirements of the ISO Standard, as evaluated by an accredited certification body, called an ISO Registrar. An ISO-certified quality manual would be a welcomed replacement for a proposal.

Think of it: A credible, no-nonsense, and indispensable management tool would replace an often contrived, superficial, and self-serving work of semi-fiction. And all those PowerPoint and "cut-and-paste" engineers could channel their efforts more productively.

In consulting circles, it's said that writing a proposal to address specifically all DoD contract requirements credibly is like trying to invent the "self-licking iced cream cone."

> **ISO certification requires nothing more than a responsible DoD contractor should be doing; and nothing more than a DoD Program Manager should expect.**

Table 14-1 summarizes (from the previous article) summarizes the readiness of four of the major ISO International Standards to address the stated operating policies of the AAF. The relationship is summarized in figure 14-1.

Table 14-1 Addressing AAF requirements with the ISO Standards

Nr	AAF Operating Policies (Ref: DoDI 5000.02)	ISO 9000 Quality Management System Clauses *	Applicable ISO Standard
1.	Simplify Acquisition Policy	Quality policies, goals, & objectives; Risk-based thinking; environmental aspects; Implementation & operation; Continual improvement; Product/process development	1,2,3,4
2.	Tailor Acquisition Approaches	Quality, policies, goals, & objectives; Operational planning & control; Design & development controls	1,2,3,4
3.	Empower Program Managers	Quality policies, goals, & objectives; Management review; Internal audit; checklist development; Communication Feedback, follow-up, & accountability;	1,2,3,4
4.	Conduct Data-driven Analysis	Quality policies, goals, & objectives; Information systems and Supply chain security management targets, data analysis & evaluation; Performance evaluation; Control of changes; Measurement and traceability	1,2,3,4
5.	Actively Manage Risk	Risk-based thinking; Quality policies, goals, & objectives; Threats, criticalities, & vulnerabilities; Establish acceptable/unacceptable risk parameters; Control of nonconforming product	1,2,3,4
6.	Emphasize Sustainment	Quality policies, goals, & objectives; Implementation & operation; Continual improvement; Nonconformity & corrective action; Preservation	1,2,3,4

ISO Standards
1. ISO 9000: Quality Management Systems
2. ISO 14000: Environmental Management Systems
3. ISO 27000: Information Security Management Systems
4. ISO 28000: Supply Chain Security Management Systems

* Note: The other three Standards have similar clauses

ISO certification requires no more than what a responsible DoD contractor should be doing anyway- and what a responsible DoD program manager should expect.

Figure 14-1 The relationship of AAF and ISO

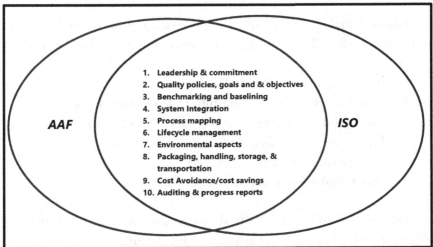

The sections that follow cover ten specific competencies necessary for successful management of DoD programs in accordance with both ISO and AAF, and in amplification of table 14-1; and how the ISO Standards (and an ISO mindset) can help to ensure the success of those programs.

1. Leadership and commitment

DoD directives require product support managers to "develop, plan, and implement a comprehensive product support strategy for all integrated product support elements and their material readiness." ISO 9001:2015 Clause 5.1 (for example) walks managers through (to name a few):

- Accountability;
- Allocation of resources;
- Roles, responsibilities, and authorities;
- Establishing policies, goals, and objectives; and
- Continual improvement.

You already know what you need to know about leadership and commitment. There is nothing new or different in the ISO Standards – just more accommodation and support.

2. *Quality policies, goals, and objectives*

Decision makers, both Military and civilian, need to establish goals and objectives for all areas of their programs, to meaningfully quantify:

- Information collection and dissemination;
- Risk, vulnerability, and the allocation of limited resources;
- Optimal data collection and reporting procedures;
- Implementation status of goals and objectives;
- Alternative courses of action; and
- Situational awareness (internal and external).

Figures 14-2 and 14-3 describe development and auditing of goals and objectives as part of the DoD acquisition big picture.

Figure 14-2 Transitioning an organization's vision into measurable goals and objectives.

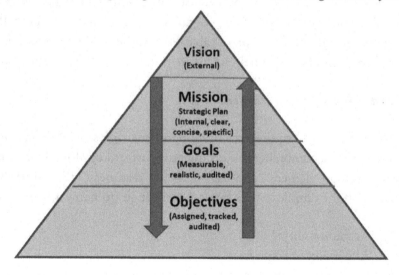

Figure 14-3 Auditing goals and objectives in the big picture

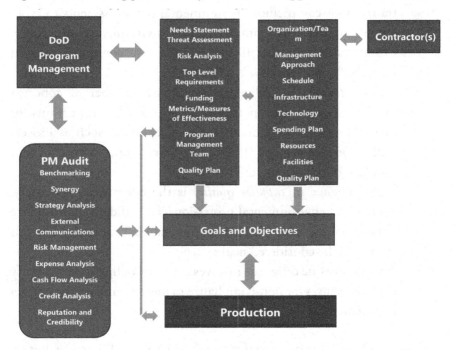

Metrics and measures of effectiveness are vital, and the metrics used to assess the effectiveness of the program can be either *subjective* (i.e., conclusions based on observations, experience, and judgment) or *objective* (based on collected data).

3. Due diligence – just "due" it

Due diligence means, essentially, to make sure that all the facts regarding an organization are available and have been independently verified. Often, in major organizations, designated due diligence "teams" consisting of financial, technical, and/or legal experts, review and analyze all operative documents and assess top management's effectiveness. I know of no such effort with DoD contracts, but strongly suggest that it be considered. In the absence of that, program managers can assess (on their own) many due diligence processes vital to contract success, to include:

- *Environmental* due diligence during commercial real estate transactions can include environmental site assessments to avoid liability under the Comprehensive Environmental Response, Compensation, and Liability Act (CERCLA), commonly referred to as the "Superfund law".
- *Manufacturing* due diligence contains a number of concepts involving either the performance of source inspections or surveillances, the performance of quality duties such as Process Validation Assessment (PVA), or system audits with a certain standard of performance.
- Due diligence in *supplier quality* is the effort made by safety, quality and environmental professionals to validate conformance of products provided by sellers to purchasers. Failure to make this effort may be considered negligence.
- *Investigative* due diligence involves a general obligation to identify true root causes for non-compliance to meet a standard or contract requirement.

The ISO Standards do not refer specifically to Due Diligence, but do provide guidance in clauses such as ISO 9001:2015 Clause 8.4: *Control of externally provided processes, products, and services.* An ISO 9000-certified contractor should be ready to provide documented, audited, proof of compliance with this clause and adherence to the many-faceted areas of due diligence.

4. System integration and connectivity

System Integration is the process of bringing together component sub-systems into one system. It is an aggregation of sub-systems cooperating so that the resultant system is able to deliver an overarching functionality or capability by ensuring that the subsystems function together as *one* system. In information technology, this is the process of linking together different computing systems and software applications physically or functionally, to act as a coordinated whole. An integrated system streamlines processes, reduces costs and increases efficiency.

The current version of ISO 9000 (ISO 9001:2015) Clause 8.5:

Production and service provision refers to product/service characteristics, results to be achieved, infrastructure, and measures of effectiveness.

Figure 14-4 describes system integration and connectivity.

Figure 14-4 System integration and connectivity

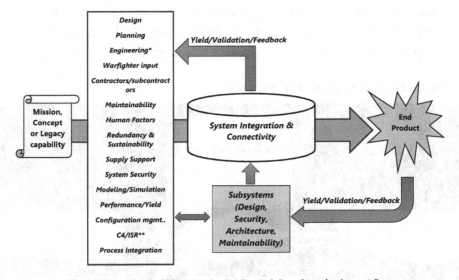

All applicable general and specialty engineering disciplines (including safety and environmental)

** Command, Control, Communications, Computers/Intelligence, Surveillance, and Reconnaissance*

The current versions of ISO 27000 and ISO 28000 (especially) address virtually every competency described in figure 4, but from a *management* perspective, so program managers are not lost in the weeds. See the legend with Table 1.

5. Process mapping

Process maps, also called "process flow charts", or (if you're old like me) "flow process charts" are graphical representations to help visualize the details of key processes and support decision making. One can identify the major areas of strengths, weaknesses, and critical paths in existing processes; and the contribution of each individual step in the process. Process maps can spotlight cycle times, redundancies, and defects.

The major components of a process map include the inputs, outputs, and the steps in the process. A good process map should illustrate the flow of the work and the interaction with the organization. It should use common language/symbols that are easily understood. An ideal process map should contain proper detail with respect to multiple paths, decisions and rework loops.

Over the years, straightforward process maps have replaced wordy quality manuals and operating procedures in the implementation of ISO-compatible processes. Figure 14-5 is an ISO-compatible process map. A comprehensive process map can replace wordy quality procedure.

Figure 14-5 A general purpose process map

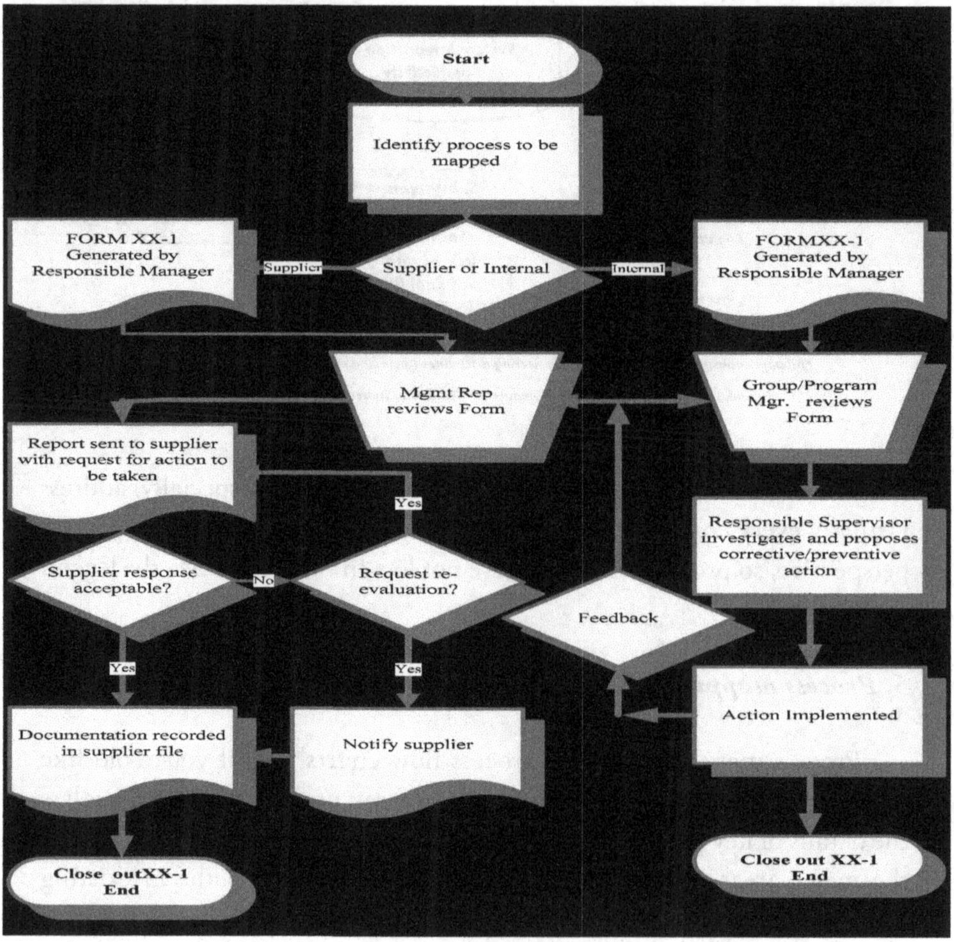

Process maps assure a contractor's understanding of the work to be done. It is virtually impossible to produce a correct process map without totally screening and understanding the process. Program managers would find it much more productive to review a contractor's process maps than his/her proposal. Process maps posted at work stations help to assure continuing adherence to specified requirements throughout the product development process. Internal auditing of the process(es) is streamlined as well.

6. Lifecycle (cradle to grave) management

Product Lifecycle Management (PLM) means managing the entire lifecycle of a product from inception, through engineering design and manufacture, to service and disposal of manufactured products in accordance with environmental requirements. DoD program managers' responsibilities don't end with the delivery of a final product (e.g.; ship or weapons system). They must plan beyond product "use" and up to and including the proper disposal of whatever is left.

Since its initial publication in 1996, ISO 14000: Environmental Management Systems, has guided forward-thinking companies though product lifecycles, and, in doing so, has taken them beyond rote environmental *compliance* and into sound environmental *management*.

7. Environmental aspects

"Environment" means the surroundings in which an organization operates, including air, water, land, natural resources, terrain, flora, fauna, and humans – individually, as communities, and as part of a global system. Every organization, public or private, large or small, needs to practice pollution prevention and energy conservation.

An environmental "aspect" is an element of an organization's activities, products, or services, with the potential to impact on the environment. A significant environmental aspect has or can have a significant environmental impact (e.g., the creation of hazardous waste as a byproduct). A process byproduct that impacts the environment, such as sandblast grit, lead-based paint, or waste oil, can stop work at that facility for an indefinite period of time and result in potential legal action against the contractor – regardless of how critical the end-product may be to the Warfighter.

Taking aboard the lessons of lifecycle management, the program manager's "cradle to grave" approach, is not just with the product itself but with the environmental aspects that surround it throughout.

ISO 14000 takes the program manager calmly but deliberately through a robust environmental management program; and, as we auditors say: "If you think having an environmental management program is expensive – try *not* having one."

8. Packaging, Handling, Storage, and Transportation

Packaging, Handling, Storage and Transportation (PHS&T) is an essential subset of DoD acquisition and logistics planning, dealing with not only the timely arrival of products to warfighters, but minimizing the risk of damage, deterioration, or corrosion enroute – even for products destined for remote, austere, and environmentally unfriendly staging areas in-theater (e.g.; the Middle East).

Robust PHS&T requirements procedures established early in product development phases promote cradle-to-grave supportability and sustainability of major end items, reparable system elements and supporting test equipment, while minimizing the impact on the environment.

Product design and development in accordance with ISO 9001:2015 Clause 8.3: *Design and development of products and services* can optimize PHS&T practices.

9. Cost avoidance and cost savings

Cost avoidance focuses on actions to avoid incurring costs *in the future*. In business, this means taking measures to lower potential increased expenses so that a company doesn't have as many costs in the future. With cost avoidance, all actions are taken to reduce future costs.

Cost *savings*, also referred to as "hard savings," means any action that lowers *current* spending, investment, or debt levels.

ISO 9001:2015: Clause 9.1.3: *Analysis and evaluation* and 9.2: *Internal*

Audit can walk program management through cost avoidance and cost savings issues as part of a product's overall performance effectiveness.

10. Auditing and progress reports

With the contract signed, the workers hired, the bonuses paid, and the empty champagne bottles removed from the conference room, DoD program managers often ask themselves: "What happens now?" "Is it done" and "have I lost my hammer?"

No. If you planned well, you should have a meaningful structure of periodic reports, allowing you to manage your program through its life.

Documentation produced in accordance with ISO Standards inevitably result in reduction of effort, volume, and redundancy. More importantly, the documentation becomes more "purposeful." "Monthly progress reports" become valuable *management tools*; as meaningless bulk and administrivia are replaced with trends, graphs, analyses, projections, and predictions; and updated EXCEL spreadsheets replace re-written, formatted, narratives – replete with dated metrics and purposes.

Assessing the readiness of a contractor to undertake a DoD contract should include assessing the ability of that contractor to effectively audit itself, and to submit to the auditing of outside registrars.

SUMMARY (Part II)

Proposals often promise a happy future by touching all the bases on the RFP. RFPs in turn reflect the vague requirements of the AAF. This could be considered "where the clouds meet the tea leaves."

Vague and/or ponderous guidance is worse than no guidance at all. ISO certification requires no more than that which a responsible DoD contractor should be doing anyway; and no more than that which a responsible DoD program manager should expect. Certification to one or more of the major ISO International Standards, as attested to by an authorized accreditation body, can (and should) replace writing and submitting proposals. Quality manuals are real; what the contractor is doing now. They predict the future by realistically and convincingly describing the present.

My recommendation remains that DoD program managers download and learn the four major ISO International Standards shown in table 1, insist upon certification by aspiring contractors, and adapt DoD program management accordingly; and within the requirements of the AAF.

Part III: The Elephant in the Room

The two primary directives of the Adaptive Acquisition Framework (AAF) are (1) DoDD 5000.01 The Defense Acquisition System (DAS); and (2) DoDI 5000.02: Operation of the Adaptive Acquisition Framework. Both are comprehensive, prescriptive, vague, and ponderous.

The DoD directives provide well-meaning but weighty guidance about "what to do," but little useful assistance regarding "*how* to do it" (or even how do you know when you *have* done it), leaving it to program managers; and word search of the following terms: "quality", "audit", "verification", and "validation" will get you: *"No matches were found"* for both directives.

This is a Part III to my previous two articles concerning the pertinency and utility of the ISO International Standards alongside the requirements of the AAF. I hope to convince readers in general and program managers in particular to implement The International Standards Organization (ISO) management standards, especially with regard to quality, environmental, information security, and supply chain security management.

These are tried, tested, updated, and ready-to-go standards, that provide structure and direction for both the creation and execution of DoD acquisition contracts – fulfilling (and clarifying) AAF requirements.

> ### We need to talk about "Politics" – the elephant in the room

However, to say the program success depends solely on the management skills of the DoD Program Manager and the technical skill of the Government Contractor is to ignore the elephant in the room. We need also to talk about "Politics" – the elephant in the room.

What do does that mean? It means that despite your most dedicated and passionate program management, your program may fall woefully short of its mission, because "politics" has forced you to lower your performance standards, in the form of capability, sustainability, cost, or delayed introduction into the Force. Your attempt to penalize, sanction, or even replace a failing contractor may be "overruled" when the contractor lobbies his side of the story to a member of Congress. You may still have a "product" or "system" (maybe even a ship) when you're done, but it won't fulfill the mission for which it was designed – and may be delivered to the scene of action too late to do any good.

Back on the home front, enthusiasm, maybe even zeal, may be replaced with a fatalistic malaise – both within DoD and the contractor. Sooner or later, even the most passionate action officer will get a set of orders and transfer (or retire). The default strategy becomes: "Let's just get it built; we'll make it work later." Like driving a new car from the dealership across the street to the repair shop.

Will the selected contractor(s) still make money? Sure. Will your civilian leadership still be satisfied? Most likely. Will analysts have something to analyze (and criticize) long after you're gone? Absolutely.

Who suffers then (or maybe dies)? The Soldier in the desert or the Sailor on the deck plate – that's who. The largest, most opulent, most prestigious offices in Washington have direct connection to those kids. DoD fails them, and we are DoD.

Beltway Botulism – an analogy

Even with the best of intentions, practices, and competencies, a DoD program is prey to what can be described as "Beltway Botulism;" a toxic and corrupting disease, which weakens, paralyzes, and poisons its victims. Here are some of Botulism's symptoms according to the Mayo Clinic:

- *Abdominal pain;*
- *Constipation, nausea, and vomiting;*
- *Dizziness and fatigue;*
- *Weak muscles and slow reflexes;*
- *Death.*

Substitute a badly prepared/managed contract for a badly prepared/managed dinner and there you have it.

The good, the bad, and the ugly

Let's start with how things should be. Our contract reflects the values of the Warfighter as well as the Executive; we have a responsible contractor and qualified (maybe certified) subcontractors; measurable milestones, and consistent, predictable, performance. Figure 14-6 summarizes what can be called "The Good." Maybe we should call it "The Perfect," because we never see it.

Figure 14-6 The Good (as in good program)

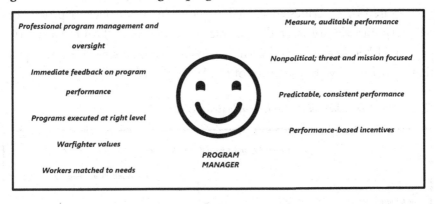

Table 14-2 summarizes program *essentials,* recommending that programs not meeting the criteria (for whatever reason) should be restructured or cancelled.

Table 14-2 Program essentials

Program Essentials	SAT: Manage it	UNSAT: Cancel it
Program commitment at the top	✓	✓
Milestones	✓	✓
Metrics (e.g., Engagement Envelope)	✓	✓
Due diligence engrained in program	✓	✓
Vision and Mission vs Reality	✓	✓
Stakeholder Influence	✓	✓
Separate/related program interference	✓	✓
Contractor competence/motivation	✓	✓
Congressional Involvement	✓	✓
Risk Management Strategy	✓	✓
Requirements analyses	✓	✓
Benchmarking/gap analyses	✓	✓
Configuration management	✓	✓
Supply chain	✓	✓
Contract Structure (Cost Plus, FFP)	✓	✓
Contractor Code of Ethics and Standards of Conduct	✓	✓
ETHICAL IMPERATIVE – ALL PARTIES	✓	✓

Instead, we often have "the Bad" as described in figure 14-7.

Figure 14-7 describes what can happen in an "atmosphere of protection" when (politically protected) contractors and "safe" DoD contracting personnel become *absorbed* with the security of their futures, and place that security above the security of the Warfighter.

Figure 14-7 The Bad (as in politically protected)

DoD directives, such as the two cited, essentially deny the existence of this complacency when they continue to suggest that the key to absolute DoD program success is to follow the guidance of those directives.

Now, let's look at figure 14-8 – the elephant in the room.

Figure 14-8 The ugly

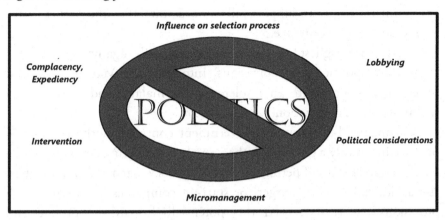

To meet today's challenges, today's Military must implement management and administrative changes that *strike a balance* with those of the major industrial organizations. Let's refer to those organizations and their environments (for now) as the "Market." Reforms to DoD practices for acquiring and managing continually improving goods and services must coincide and support, without being subservient to, those of the Market. Continuous improvement programs, structures, and standardizations, such as the ISO Family of International Standards bring the Military and the Market together well; allowing both to focus on the common goal of Mission Accomplishment.

> ## *Military + Market = Mission*
> ## *(Maybe)*

The all-too-frequent problem occurs when the DoD – Contractor relationship is sidestepped by either the Contractor or members of Congress (and their staffs). Contractors, who themselves are often a mosaic of ambitious smaller entities seeking a piece of the pie, dispatch lobbyists to remind Congressmen that the work in question (and in jeopardy) is being done in their districts. As a result, DoD is often told to reaffirm its support for the contract – however precarious it may have become.

Another problem for DoD comes from *within*, when bureaucrats, comfortable in their positions, reenforce the status quo. They do this by refusing to modernize procedures to conform with modern management or administration, or to support calls for accountability and proper award for measurable performance.

DoD, at the highest level, must stand (externally) against the pervasive intrusion of politics (and politicians) into Program Management; and (internally) demonstrate an intolerance for malaise and complacency within its own organization.

Companies bult around a government contract (or the promise of one) are inherently a greater risk than an already-existing company with a credible track record of performance. Contracts written as Small Business "set-asides" are an easy target for start-up companies; and, while such provisions may satisfy a need, they potentially jeopardize a product and the Warfighter using it. Lowering the bar of performance is written in to the contract; and that's no way to treat the Military.

In the book: _Keeping the Edge – Managing Defense for the Future_, Ashton Carter, John P. White (Ed), and a host of experts, advanced the DoD cause by stating areas wherein members of Congress and their professional staffs can help as well as where their involvement is detrimental. The book also suggests where Federal Acquisition Regulations (FAR) need to recognize and act in accordance with the "Market." That is: where the most competent, most professional, contractors may be found, and how they can work together.

Figure 14-9 takes some of the book's recommendations and summarizes them; optimally reflecting DoD _and_ contractor requirements in an atmosphere of trust and cooperation.

Figure 14-9 Working together in trust and cooperation

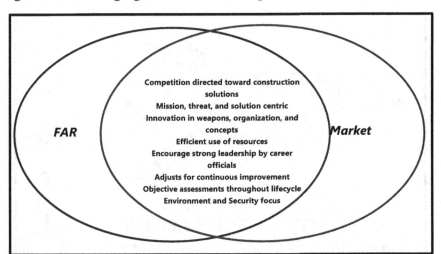

The concepts and practices listed inside the two circles need no explanation to program managers. They do, in total, comprise a *state* or a *condition* which program managers strive to achieve, contractors should perceive as a "win-win," and Warfighters have every right to expect.

Figure 14-10 suggests further that program success comes sooner when DoD and the Government contractors each recognize how they can best work together toward the goals and objectives of the mission; and that senior DoD personnel need to develop training and contracts with which both sides can operate optimally.

Figure 14-10 The Goal

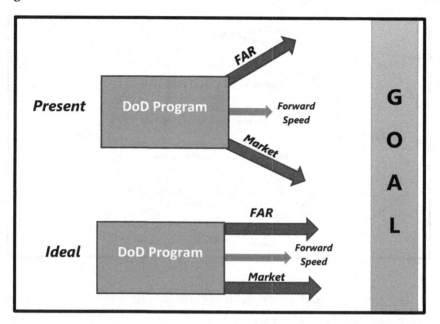

You can get where you're going faster and sooner, if both of your feet are pointed in the same direction.

SUMMARY

A DoD program will, in some way, fail if the essential requirements described in table 1 are not met. A program manager can present justification for a *decision* to cancel. The *courage* to cancel after that decision has to be supported through the DoD chains of command to the top, if necessary.

Ashton Carter's book remains (in my opinion) a compendium of definitive guidance for transforming DoD program management and all the training and direction that goes with it, in order to strike a balance with credible, ethical, and success-oriented industrial organizations.

DoD, at the highest level, must take a stand against the pervasive intrusion of politics (and politicians) into DoD Acquisition Management; and to demonstrate an intolerance for malaise and complacency within its own organization. "Take a stand" is the operative phrase. It's too late for *squishy* words like "support" or "encourage."

Lastly, and as I continue to recommend, put this sign over your desk:

> *"The only thing necessary for evil to triumph*
> *is for good men to do nothing."*
> *Edmund Burke (1729 - 1797)*

CHAPTER FIFTEEN

Tainted and counterfeit products – Something else for program managers to deal with, and right away

The ability to monitor, predict, plan for, and react to *overt* cyber-attack is vital – both on the battlefield and in the office. So also, is the ability to uncover *covert* tainted and counterfeit components in commercial off the shelf (COTS) products – initially and throughout the product's lifecycle.

When DoD or one of its contractors is not prepared for cyber-attack, or has an inadequate contingency plan in place, disruption and disaster follows. Military and civilian organizations have seen firsthand the vulnerability of business systems, operations, and revenue streams, to overt and covert cyber-attack, or witnessed the critical importance of risk awareness and preparedness; and thus understand the need for robust risk and continuity management programs. DoD needs precise management programs (inside larger management programs) focused directly on the detection, preclusion, or removal of tainted or counterfeit components in its systems.

A *tainted* product is a product that is produced by the provider and is acquired through a provider's authorized supply chain but has been tampered with maliciously. A *counterfeit* product is produced other than by or for the provider, or is supplied by other than a provider's authorized channel, but is still represented as legitimate. For example, a provider could source a product from a supplier that purports to be from the correct vendor, but is, instead, a "fake".

Counterfeit products pose significant risks to because the integrity of a fake product cannot be validated. In addition, counterfeit (or illegitimate) products are not supported by legitimate providers, and can result in significant financial, productivity, or mission losses. This degrades and possibly endangers the warfighter, whose counterfeit product may fail at a critical juncture. Similarly, the supplier, whose revenue stream and brand are damaged due to a fake/counterfeit product. Even in cases where the fake is a nearly authentic copy of the original, the mission may be damaged by the inability to get support. Contractors and subcontractors are damaged by loss of revenue stream that should rightly accrue from their intellectual property.

ISO 20242:2018

The International Organization for Standardization (ISO) developed ISO 20243:2018: *The Open Trusted Technology Provide Standard (O-TTPS)*. It provides guidelines, recommendations, and requirements, to help assure against maliciously tainted and counterfeit products in commercial off-the-shelf (COTS) information and communication technology (ICT) product lifecycles.

I have been writing recently (and for over 20 years) about the measurable benefits to be gained by aggressively incorporating selected ISO Standards into developing and implementing DoD contracts. Toward that end, I unhesitatingly recommend adding ISO 20243:2018, as:

- A specific contract requirement for contracts involving COTS components;
- A stated subset of one of the major ISO Standards, such as ISO 9001:2015: *Quality Management Systems*; or
- Unofficial guidance for DoD program managers and contract developers and auditors, in order to protect against the potential for tainted or counterfeit products or components.

This Standard, if implemented by DoD and its contractors, will measurably reduce the sourcing risks that can introduce tainted, low-quality, or counterfeit products or components. Proactive, security-conscious, organizations adapt and periodically assess sourcing strategies and best practices in accordance with this Standard.

ISO 20243:2018/O-TTPS integrates highly effectively with the better-known ISO Standards. Table 15-1 describes the compatibility of O-TTPS with better known international standards.

Table 15-1 ISO 20243 compatibility with other ISO Standards

Requirement	ISO 9000	ISO 27000	ISO 28000	ISO 20243
Standards and Explanation	x	x	x	x
Top management involvement	x	x	x	x
Employee ownership, training, responsibility	x	x	x	x
Reflected in Strategic Plan	x	x	x	x
Process Oriented	x	x	x	x
Documentation required	x	x	x	x
Manual and checklists for structure	x	x	x	x
Capable of self-audit or certification	x	x	x	x
Consolidates other standards and requirements	x	x	x	x
Feedback and preventive actions generated	x	x	x	x
Focused training and qualification program	x	x	x	x

Note: ISO 9001: 2015: Quality Management Systems; ISO 27001: 2007: Information Systems Security Management Systems; ISO 28001: Supply Chain Security Management Systems.

O-TTPS takes the guidance and direction of the Information Security and Supply Chain Security Management and focuses on the secure development and movement of products, the risks associated with both, and the ability to detect and counter low-quality or counterfeit components or sub-products.

All of these International Standards are available on the internet for immediate download, instruction, and guidance.

ASSESSMENT GUIDANCE

This Standard provides assessment guidance regarding:

- Best practices by the best companies;
- The business rationale for why a DoD contractor implemented this Standard and why it is becoming certified;
- What personnel should understand about the Certification Program and how they can best develop and maintain their processes;
- The differences between the options (self-assessed or third-party assessed) that are currently available for the Certification Program; and
- The process steps and the terms and conditions of the certification, with pointers to the relevant supporting documents, which are freely available.

Protecting against threats from outside the contractor's control

The Standard addresses threats that originate *outside* a DoD contractor's normal span of control. For example, a counterfeiter producing a fake printed circuit board assembly with no original linkage to the Original Equipment Manufacturer (OEM). The practices detailed in the Assessment offer as great a level of mitigation as possible. An example is the use of security labeling techniques in legitimate products.

ACTIVITIES FOR ASSESSMENT AND CERTIFICATION

The O-TTPS framework requires candidates seeking certification to implement its control requirements across three layers: (1) product development; (2) secure engineering; and (3) supply chain security. The Standard includes best practices throughout all phases of a product's life cycle. Specifically: design, sourcing, build, fulfillment, distribution, sustainment, and disposal; thereby (internally) enhancing the integrity of COTS products and (externally) the security of their global supply chains.

The areas of specific focus and control, referred to as "Assessor Activities" in the O-TTPS are listed in the yellow oval in figure 15-1.

Figure 15-1 ISO Standards and Assessor Activities

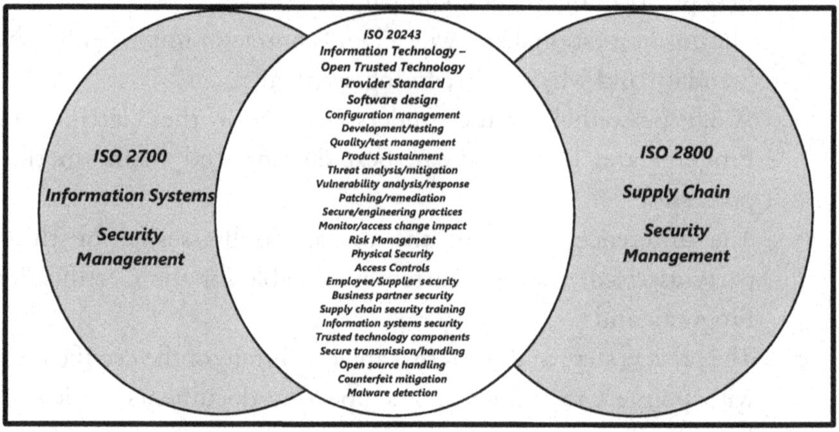

ISO 20243
Information Technology –
Open Trusted Technology
Provider Standard
Software design
Configuration management
Development/testing
Quality/test management
Product Sustainment
Threat analysis/mitigation
Vulnerability analysis/response
Patching/remediation
Secure/engineering practices
Monitor/access change impact
Risk Management
Physical Security
Access Controls
Employee/Supplier security
Business partner security
Supply chain security training
Information systems security
Trusted technology components
Secure transmission/handling
Open source handling
Counterfeit mitigation
Malware detection

ISO 2700
Information Systems
Security
Management

ISO 2800
Supply Chain
Security
Management

ASSESSMENT TARGETS, OBJECTIVES, AND RESOURCES

An initial step in the assessment is to determine the scope of the O-TTPS implementation (How much); the projected completion date of the effort (when); the required level of personnel expertise and financial resources (how much).

The objectives of the O-TTPS are:

a. To reduce the risk of acquiring maliciously tainted or counterfeit products;

b. To document best practices derived from the experience of mature industry providers;

c. Establish requirements and recommendations to provide significant advantage in reducing risk;

d. To use specific methodologies to assure the hardware or software of COTS Information and ICT products;

e. To develop conformance criteria, and assessment procedures;

f. To establish and operate a meaningful, and replicable certification process; and to ensure that an alignment of interests exists between public and Government customers.

Table 15-2 is an example of turning a routine monthly report into a dynamic, auditable, management tool for tracking targets and objectives. I continue to recommend this approach.

Table 15-2 A goals and objectives (EXCEL) worksheet

GOALS AND OBJECTIVES					
Goal I. Protect all Information against Unauthorized Access					
Objective	Description	Assigned	Completion Date	Remarks	
I-1	Revise all passwords 1/qtr	FSO; DHs	31-Dec-17	Quarterly thereafter	**Notes:** Goals - Objectives - Plan of Action & Milestones
I-2	Test all Intrusion alarms 2x/yr	FSO	31-Dec-17		Tracking numbers, not bullets
I-3	Conduct Annual Security Training	FSO; DHs	31-Dec-17	All employees sign on completion	Action statement, not conditional/passive voice
					Responsibilities assigned
					Completion dates
					Track at Management Review meetings

The table, when used as a management tool, becomes top management's Plan of Action and Milestones (POA&M).

EVIDENCE OF CONFORMANCE

There are many security mechanisms that may be used and referenced in the "Evidence of Conformance" section: e.g.; digital signatures, encryption, hashing, and bound mechanisms. Assessment records should contain supplementary information (as appropriate) about the assessment methodology used for each requirement.

Certification provides DoD with formal recognition of a contractor's conformance to the O-TTPS, which allows practitioners to make and substantiate clear claims of conformance to the Standard, and acquirers to specify and successfully procure from providers who conform to the Standard.

Table 15-3 contains several the assessment activities, the compliance requirements, and the source of evidence confirming the activities' proper operation and management.

Table 15-3 An assessment activities checklist (one page)

Type*	Activity	Requirement	Evidence	In-Place Y/N/Date
PE/IE	4.1 Software/Firmware Design Process	A process to ensure requirements are addressed in the design	Product requirement management process	
			Design artifacts Traceability report Audit report Product reqm'ts doc.	
PE/IE	4.2 Configuration Management	A formal Configuration Management process document A formal Change Management process	Configuration Change Mgmt docs. All assets and artifacts identified; baselines established	
		Product baselines track and control process	Products tracked and controlled	
			Problem reports; change reviews; scope reviews	
		Protect and secure access to identified assets, artifacts, and supporting systems	Access control policy; Audit reports; sign-in docs	
		A formal acceptance criteria document, process, and/or baseline	Acceptance reports	
PE/IE	4.3 Well-defined Development/Engineering Method Processes and Practices	Documented engineering practices and processes	Ability to track proven targets of tainting and counterfeiting throughout life cycle	
		Documented product development process	Component labeling throughout life cycle	

Prepared:_____ Date:_____

Approved:_____ Date:_____

Type of Evidence Conformance:		
I.E.	Implementation Evidence	Artifacts that show that the required process has been applied to the selected representative products
P.E.	Process Evidence	The evidence/artifacts listed as required to demonstrate that the required processes/procedures have been defined

My actual spreadsheet is seven (landscape) pages. Contact me and I will send you the complete version. The addition of one (or more) additional columns, remarks, assignments, dates, and signatures, make an otherwise static checklist into a dynamic plan of action and milestones. Maintaining it as a spreadsheet makes review, update, and distribution, easy, and creates a valuable management tool.

RISK MANAGEMENT STRATEGY

As overt and covert cyber-attacks increase in sophistication, stealth, and severity, global governments and larger enterprises have also begun to take a more comprehensive approach to *risk management* as it applies to product integrity and supply chain security. In addition to enhancing information security by improving security practices across the supply chains (the focus of ISO Standards 27000 and 28000) both DoD and its contractors are inquiring more frequently into the practices COTS vendors' actions to protect the integrity of their products and services as they are developed and enter the global supply chain. The assessment activities contained in the Standard highlight specific risks associated with tainted and counterfeit COTS and ICT products.

As with any DoD program/sub-program, O-TTPS requires a repeatable methodology for risk assessment and management, in order to identify and mitigate gaps in the processes; and to determine at what point risks become unacceptable.

Figure 15-2 is a graph from a notional risk management spreadsheet model, prepared in accordance with ISO 20243. The blue bars represent the risks identified and assessed; and the red bars describe the same risks after some (notional) form of mitigation.

Figure 15-2 Graph from a risk management spreadsheet model

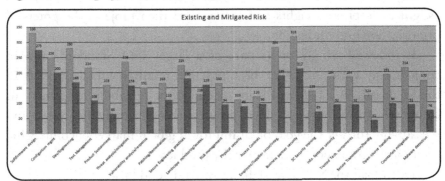

When identifying and assessing risks, program managers should also identify and quantify (as possible) potential corrections or mitigations for those risks. It is at that point, as I have said before, that *risk assessment* becomes *risk management.*

SUMMARY

There is a clear difference between the variety of supply chain business risks (e.g., a supplier going out of business or selling a bad product) and targeted supply chain attacks (e.g., maliciously corrupting a component within a product being sold). Two of the primary targeted attack areas are tainted and counterfeit products. DoD and contractors should be very concerned about the danger from these attacks.

To implement and optimize ISO 20243 in DoD contracts is to identify and mitigate supply chain risks specifically associated with overt or covert attacks on the DoD supply chain before they happen. An attendant focus on the use of best practices in these critical areas leads to the improvements that both DoD and contractors want; plus, mission accomplishment, warfighter safety, and an improved global market.

Recognizing COTS realities and given the continual improvement in vulnerability analysis tools and techniques, this Standard identifies best practice requirements and recommendations in COTS – related areas of risk to the supply chain.

O-TTPS contains, within itself, a robust and realistic risk management strategy, in which it identifies threats, criticalities, and vulnerabilities, assigns appropriate weights and values, and then projects the potential prioritization and mitigation.

If followed, singly or as part of a larger ISO Standard, and in conjunction with the other best practice requirements identified in the Standard, O-TTPS will help to reduce the possibility of tainted or counterfeit intrusion as products progress through their life cycles, and measurably further the goal of an improved global market encompassing trustworthy suppliers and trustworthy products.

Download the Standard right away. And good luck.

CHAPTER SIXTEEN

Auditing Computer-Based Information Security – Gain Control and Keep it

> *We remain incredibly uneducated, unstructured, and vulnerable, when it comes to threats to the security of our information systems.*

DoD and, for that matter, every one of us, is in danger of physical or cyber-attack, because we remain incredibly uneducated, unstructured, and vulnerable, when it comes to threats to our security. DoD must *harden* and enforce its contracts – at their creation and fully throughout their life cycles. Our organizational security must be upgraded profoundly and continuously, through a robust program of internal and outside information security audits.

An "audit" is a systematic, independent, and documented process for obtaining evidence and evaluating it objectively, in order to determine the extent to which audit criteria have been fulfilled. *Information systems auditing* is the process of collecting and evaluating evidence to determine whether or not a computer system safeguards assets and resources, maintains data integrity, allows organizational goals to be achieved effectively, and uses resources efficiently. More on this in the sections that follow.

INFORMATION CONTROL

> *"Information is the only weapon that can be in more than one place at the same time." - Somebody smart*
> *"No good decision can come from bad data." – Me*

DoD information systems process data and provide decision-making information – in the office, the laboratory, and the battlespace. Because of the focus and determination of those aggressors who would do us harm, it is vital that our information security be under the tightest, most rigorous control possible. Control also means compliance with legal, statutory, and other regulatory security requirements, security management objectives, delivery of secure products, and security throughout the supply chain.

Loss (or ineffective) control of computer information systems control can result in:

- Destruction, theft, or modification of resources
- Privacy violations
- Disruption of operations
- Physical harm to personnel.

Data is a critical resource, necessary for virtually all of DoD's missions and operations in an ever-changing environment. Lost or corrupted data, or correct data in the hands of the aggressor, can lead to loss of mission and loss of life. Decisions made as the result of bad data can be disastrous.

AUDIT OBJECTIVES

In his seminal book *Information Systems Control and Audit*, University of Queensland Professor Ron Weber cites four major objectives of information systems auditing, as follows.

1. Safeguarding of resources.

"Resources" are hardware, software, facilities, people, data files, system documentation and integrators, and supplies. These can be destroyed maliciously, stolen or destroyed, and/or used for unauthorized purposes. They may be concentrated in a limited number of locations; in some cases, one single disk. Physically safeguarding these personnel, spaces, and equipment is both basic and essential to an organization's security management system.

2. Improved data integrity

"Data integrity" is a condition or state implying that data has completeness, soundness, purity, and veracity. If data integrity is not (or no longer) maintained, the command, program, or mission no longer has a true and accurate representation of itself or its operations. Resultant is loss of mission effectiveness or program control. Data integrity, or the loss thereof is often described in terms of its impact on decision-making effectiveness, information sharing, and its value to opposing forces.

3. Improved system effectiveness

Auditing and evaluating system effectiveness require that auditors know exactly the objectives of the systems. The information gathered and processed must satisfy the collection and decision-making objectives for which it is being managed. For this reason, auditing must take place starting at the design stages, at implementation, and repeatedly, to ensure goals are being met and opportunities for improvement are identified.

4. Improved system efficiency

System *effectiveness*, as described above, is measured using a variety of metrics. System *efficiency* means that the system is using minimal resources to reach the required level of effectiveness.

AUDIT MANAGEMENT

> *"Things refuse to be mismanaged for long" - Ralph Waldo Emerson*

I am not in the habit of quoting Emerson. However, I can't help but agree with this statement.

Years ago, one of my many and often-frustrated (by me) mentors had a sign over his desk which read: *"Expect What You Inspect."* That meant (as he patiently explained): (1) that if you check on something routinely, before long you will be happy with what you see; (2) if you hardly ever check, you will not be happy, and will be forced to look at it and to fix it; and (3) that if you inspect frequently, then the area not only functions well, but continues to improve.

Looking critically at internal functions and processes and comparing findings with approved standards is the basis of the audit. An organization can audit itself, or hire an independent auditor/consultant, or a combination of both. As a result, internal (self) and external (e.g., by a registrar) audits give organizations comprehensive self-sustaining evaluation and improvement capability.

Figure 16-1 describes an effective information security management strategy for both internal and external audits.

Figure 16-1 Conducting and managing information security aud

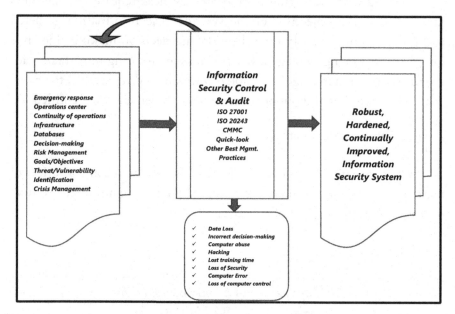

Organizations don't always do all the work required for effective audits, nor do they adequately qualify internal auditors. As a result, audits tend to be sporadic, biased, and perfunctory. More important, critical findings of the type discussed herein, may not be uncovered, and corrective actions not initiated.

Instead of executing a meaningful measure of organization security and effectiveness, unqualified or unmotivated auditors only waste time, annoy busy people, and turn off top management to the potential benefits of internal auditing.

DoD contracts are only now starting to require auditing to international standards, but thus far only in a superficial "check this block" manner. It is up to program managers not only to demand these standards in their contracts, but to make sure they are scrupulously implemented. And audited. The good news is that program managers can start immediately, by auditing their programs on their own, in accordance with the guidance provided herein and readily available off the internet. Why wait?

INTERNATIONAL AUDITING STANDARDS FOR INFORMATION SECURITY

Checklist ➤ *Audit Report* ➤ *POA&M*

I have written previously for DAU (and for many years before that) about the potential *value-add* of structured information systems security management standards like ISO 27000 and ISO 20243 (Parts 1 and 2). I have audited both public and private sector organizations to these standards with very substantial results.

Table 16-1 lists three proven, readily-available, and high value, international standards for auditing information systems security. They are all available on the internet for immediate download. When implemented, the standards can measurably upgrade and continuously improve the security of any DoD information system, contract, program, or mission.

Table 16-1 Three readily available International Standards for auditing and managing Information Security

Designation	Title	Self-Audit	Certification	Available now on the net
ISO 27001-2013	Information Systems Security Management	x	x	x
ISO 24243 – 1 (Pts 1 & 2)	Open Trusted Technology Provider Standard (O-TTPS)	x	x	x
CMMC	Cybersecurity Maturity Model Certification	x	x	x

The International Organization for Standardization (ISO) developed *ISO 27000* to provide the requirements for establishing, implementing, maintaining, and continually improving an information security management system within an organization.

ISO 20243:2018: *The Open Trusted Technology Provide Standard (O-TTPS)* provides guidelines, recommendations, and requirements against maliciously tainted and counterfeit products in commercial off-the-shelf (COTS) information and communication technology (ICT) product lifecycles.

Now, I want to introduce Cybersecurity Maturity Model Certification, or "CMMC". Auditing a program or organization for CMMC compliance means reviewing existing policies and network diagrams, and conducting scoping interviews to examine how controlled information flows into, within, and from an organization. At the same time, a CMMC audit assesses the *maturity* of those controls (e.g., how strong they are and how equal to future tasks and challenges). The information gained from the audit creates, revises, and continuously improves an organization's CMMC System Security Plan.

The guidance in the CMMC standard can be (at times) cumbersome and repetitive. However, it is better to start with too much guidance and tailor it to what you need, rather than to have too little guidance and overlook the security of a critical process or sub-process. You can develop a checklist tailored to the mission, and, in doing so, make an arguably problematic requirements document it to an effective management tool.

Figure 16-2 is a small section of a CMMC checklist which I developed on an EXCEL spreadsheet, and made into a combination checklist and "stoplight chart". Readers are welcome to contact me for the complete spreadsheet.

Figure 16-2 A "completed" section of a CMMC checklist/stoplight chart

3.3.7 Provide a capability that compares and synchronizes internal system clocks to generate time stamps for audit records.			
Assessed	**Where to Look:**	**Assessment**	**Comment**
12-Dec	• audit and accountabilitypolicy		Update
12-Dec	• procedures addressing time stamp generation information		
12-Dec	• system design documentation		Corect ASAP
12-Dec	• information system configuration settings and associated documentation		Revise
12-Dec	• information system audit records		
12-Dec	• other relevant documents or records		
	Who to Talk to:		
12-Dec	• employees with information security responsibilities		
12-Dec	• system/network administrators		Re-train
12-Dec	• systemdevelopers		
	Perform Test On:		
12-Dec	• automated mechanisms implementing time stamp generation		Test again
12-Dec	automated mechanisms implementing internal information system sclock synchronization		Reclibrate

The colored-in boxes make for an efficient audit debriefing vehicle. Additional columns with headings such as "Objective Number," "Assigned," and/or "Completion Date" may be added, in order to turn the audit report quickly into an *actionable* plan of action & milestones, or POA&M.

"QUICK-LOOKS"

Quick-looks are immediate, high pay-back, self-audits that forward-thinking program and security managers can use to reduce the vulnerability and attractiveness of their facilities to physical or cyber-attack.

Table 16-2 A simple quick-look checklist

Designation	Quick-look	Date	SAT/ UNSAT	Remarks
I-1	Intrusion Detection Systems			
I-2	Fences, Security lighting, natural barriers			
I-3	CCTV			
I-4	Computer backup systems; firewalls			
I-5	Roof and ventilator duct accessibility			
I-6	Construction materials/thickness requirements			
I-7	Roads and alleys			
I-8	Parking areas			
I-9	Locks, doors and access control			
I-10	Identification management			
I-11	Utilities (including uninterruptible power systems)			
I-12	Safes, desks, file cabinets. Controlled/exclusion areas			
I-13	Hazmat generation and management			
I-14	Vehicle surveillance/security			
I-15	Proximity of emergency services			
I-16	Mail and package processing			

Prepared/Date _____

Reviewed/Date_____

SUMMARY

DoD must *harden* and enforce its contracts – at their creation and throughout their life cycles. Instead of executing a meaningful measure of organization security and effectiveness, unqualified or unmotivated auditors only waste time, annoy busy people, and turn off top management to the potential benefits of internal auditing.

Everything program managers need for robust, cradle-to-grave; information systems security management is available *right now* on the internet. It remains only for them to download, tailor, and implement; and to make the standards their own.

Developing a real information security strategy, using the standards and checklists immediately available on the net, and taking action on your findings will improve the security posture of your program or operation – immediately and continuously; potentially saving a program, mission, and who knows what else. The success of Information Security in DoD is the result of the corrective and preventive actions that DoD Management takes as the result of audits and their findings.

DoD needs to make Information Security Management part of every program, organization, and mission, and then approach it like any other:

- Establish open communication and feedback loops;
- Establish policies and procedures; conduct gap analyses and risk assessments;
- Implement processes;
- Identify corrective and preventive actions, lessons learned and training requirements;
- Establish a mindset of continuous improvement; and
- Audit, audit, audit.

Make a checklist like table 16-2 for your organization and fill it in by the end of the week. You'll be glad you did.

> ### *Closing thought"*
>
> *The same measuring criteria that <u>support</u> a good program <u>indict</u> a bad one. The ethical imperative, that discomforting reminder to leaders and managers that when lives are at stake you either make the program work or make it go away, is both timeless and universal.*

Good luck, and now let's get to work.

Other books by Gene Razzetti:

1. *The Executive's Guide to Corporate Responsibility Management and MVO 8000 (2nd Ed)*
2. *Fixes That Last – The Executive's Guide to Fix It or Lose It Management (2nd Ed)*
3. *The Executive's Guide to Internal Auditing*
4. *Hardening by Auditing (Revision in progress)*
5. *The Executive's Guide to Creating and Implementing an Integrated Management System*

All books are available hard copy or electronically through all the usual channels.

ABOUT THE AUTHOR

 Eugene A. (Gene) Razzetti retired from the U.S. Navy as a Captain in 1992, a Vietnam Veteran and having had two at-sea and two major shore commands. Since then, he has been an independent management consultant, project manager, and ISO auditor. He became an adjunct military analyst with the Center for Naval Analyses after September 11, 2001. He has authored five management books, numerous articles for professional journals, and co-authored MVO 8000, an international Corporate Responsibility Management (Ethics) Standard. He has served on boards and committees dealing with ethics and professionalism in the practice of management consulting. He is a senior member of the American Society for Quality (ASQ) and assisted the Government of Guatemala with markedly heightening the environmental and security postures of its two principal commercial port facilities.

He can be reached at www.corprespmgmt.com or generazz@aol.com.

Printed in the United States
by Baker & Taylor Publisher Services